CHOOSING A P

How To Books for Family Reference

Applying for Legal Aid
Arranging Insurance
Becoming a Father
Buying a Personal Computer
Caring for Someone at Home
Cash from Your Computer
Choosing a Nursing Home
Choosing a Package Holiday
Dealing with a Death in the Family
Having a Baby
How to Apply to an Industrial
  Tribunal
How to be a Local Councillor
How to be an Effective School
  Governor
How to Claim State Benefits
How to Lose Weight & Keep Fit

How to Make a Wedding Speech
How to Plan a Wedding
How to Raise Funds & Sponsorship
How to Run a Local Campaign
How to Run a Voluntary Group
How to Survive Divorce
How to Take Care of Your Heart
How to Use the Internet
Making a Complaint
Making a Video
Managing Your Personal Finances
Successful Grandparenting
Successful Single Parenting
Taking in Students
Teaching Someone to Drive
Winning Consumer Competitions

Other titles in preparation

The How To series now contains more than 200 titles in the following
categories:

Business Basics
Family Reference
Jobs and Careers
Living and Working Abroad
Student Handbooks
Successful Writing

Please send for a free copy of the latest catalogue for full details
(see back cover for address).

FAMILY REFERENCE

CHOOSING A PACKAGE HOLIDAY

How to plan and prepare
for a disaster-free experience

Christine Miller

How To Books

Cartoons by Mike Flanagan

British Library Cataloguing in Publication Data
A catalogue record for this book is available from the British Library.

© Copyright 1997 by Christine Miller.

First published in 1997 by How To Books Ltd, Plymbridge House,
Estover Road, Plymouth PL6 7PZ, United Kingdom. Tel: (01752) 202301.
Fax: (01752) 202331.

Produced for How To Books by Deer Park Productions.

Typeset by Concept Communications (Design & Print) Ltd, Crayford, Kent.
Printed and bound by Cromwell Press, Broughton Gifford, Melksham, Wiltshire.

Contents

List of Illustrations

Preface

Your holiday is one of your biggest annual expenditures, yet it is the only product which you cannot inspect or sample before purchasing, and often your only guide to making your choice is a glossy brochure and biased information.

There are plenty of resort guides available once you have chosen your destination, but very little information on the technicalities of choosing your destination and booking your holiday.

This book is designed to put you in the picture before you enter the travel agency, so that you are in control and can advise the travel agent of your requirements, and so reduce the risk of being talked into buying an unsuitable holiday. Whilst travel agents do provide useful advice, sometimes the information they give is biased. The book also highlights the areas where they are under pressure to sell certain products.

Each chapter guides you through the booking process with case studies featuring three sets of characters. Many of the situations are drawn from my eleven years' experience in working in travel agencies.

No matter which destination you choose, I hope this book will guide you in the direction of a disaster-free holiday.

Christine Miller

IS THIS YOU?

Student

Course lecturer

Training board

Teacher

First time traveller

Seasoned traveller

Senior citizen

Family with children

Family with teenagers

Single person

School leaver

Group leader

Teenager

Special interest group

Couple

Sports club leader

Social club leader

Landlord

Youth club leader

Holidaymaker

Expatriate

Wife

Husband

Club secretary

Travel agent

Honeymooner

Hotelier

Backpacker

Graduate

Sightseer

Businessperson

Parent

1
Understanding the Brochures

CALCULATING THE BASIC COSTS

Anyone who has spent time looking at holiday brochures will know that they are not the most straightforward of documents. Some information is on one page, some is at the back of the brochure; it can be confusing and frustrating trying to marry up all the relevant information, as well as understanding what all the codes and descriptions mean, not to mention arriving at the right costing for the holiday.

As it is important to understand all aspects of your proposed holiday, this chapter explains how to arrive at the correct cost for it. It is easy to forget to add on the supplements which can make a substantial difference to the overall holiday total. On arrival at the travel agents you could discover, after many hours poring over the brochures, that your holiday choice is well out of your price range.

Arriving at a basic hotel price

A basic hotel price is the one which appears on the pricing grid in the brochure before any supplements are added.

The larger tour operators – for example Thomson, Cosmos, Airtours – have a similar layout to their brochures, in that the basic prices are listed on the same page as the hotel description. Flight information and supplements are normally found at the back of the brochure.

To arrive at a basic hotel price:

1. Find the pricing grid relevant to your chosen hotel, usually on the same page as the hotel description.

2. Cross reference the departure date, usually on the left hand side of the grid, against the number of nights you want to spend in the hotel.

3. Where the two boxes meet will give you the basic price.

At the side of the pricing grid, the days on which flights operate from regional airports are usually listed. Your departure date must match up with

11

Accommodation & meal arrangements:	Tropical Beach				
	Half board				
Flights available:	Tues Fri and Sun only				
Accommodation code:	ZPW				
Prices based on:	pb wc bl				
Number of nights:	7	10	11	14	All
Adult/child	Adult	Adult	Adult	Adult	1st child
23 Apr-9 May	241	312	351	413	139
10 May-17 May	274	337	376	441	149
18 May-24 May	311	386	415	483	189
25 May-30 May	365	438	467	525	209
31 May-13 Jun	324	409	433	521	169
14 Jun-22 Jun	335	434	468	543	179
23 Jun-7 Jul	361	459	487	559	199
8 Jul-13 Jul	377	482	515	581	209
14 Jul-20 Jul	386	481	523	595	249
21 Jul-9 Aug	409	513	527	616	269
10 Aug-17 Aug	387	492	526	606	269
18 Aug-22 Aug	385	481	513	584	269
23 Aug-29 Aug	381	469	497	592	239
30 Aug-10 Sep	378	456	472	569	209
11 Sep-26 Sep	365	430	463	549	169
27 Sep-8 Oct	325	381	417	490	159
9 Oct-17 Oct	281	340	383	441	149
18 Oct-29 Oct	279	338	371	–	159

Supplements per person per night: Single room £8.10 Sea view £3.60
Full board £5.15

Reductions per person per night: 3rd/4th adult only sharing £6.35

☐ Edward's and Jean's holiday costing ⎫
◯ Nancy's holiday costing   ⎬ see case studies
                                 ⎭

Fig. 1. Sample hotel pricing grid.

12

a day of the week on which flights depart from your chosen regional airport. If this is not checked and the next nearest alternative falls into a higher price on the grid, it could make a big difference to the overall cost.

Figure 1 shows a sample hotel pricing grid and Figure 2 shows a sample flight availability chart.

Flights available from:		
Gatwick	:	Tues, Fri, Sat
Luton	:	Tues, Fri, Sat
Stanstead	:	Fri, Sat
Bristol	:	Fri
Cardiff	:	Sun
Birmingham	:	Tues, Sun
Manchester	:	Tues, Fri, Sun
Newcastle	:	Tues, Sun
Glasgow	:	Fri, Sun

Fig. 2. Sample flight availability chart.

Arriving at a basic self catering price

A basic self catering price is the one which appears on the pricing grid before any supplements are added.

Again, the larger tour operators tend to list their basic prices on the same page as the apartment description, with flight information and supplements at the back of the brochure.

The costing for self catering holidays does differ from hotel holidays in that the prices depend on the number of people sharing accommodation.

Generally you will find three types of self catering accommodation on offer:

- studios – which take 2–3 people
- one bedroomed apartments – which take 2-4 people
- two bedroomed apartments – which take 4-6 people.

To arrive at a basic self catering price:

1. Find the pricing grid relevant to your chosen studio/apartment.

2. Decide upon the size of studio/apartment which best suits your party.

3. Cross reference the departure date against the size of studio/apartment and number of nights you want to stay.

4. Where the two boxes meet will give you the basic price.

Accommodation & meal arrangements:	Montenova Apartments									
	Self catering									
Flights available:	Tues Fri Sun flights only									

Accommodation code:	CZB				CZA				All	
Prices based on:	1 bed apt 4 adults				2 bed apt 6 adults				apt types children	
Number of nights	7	10	11	14	7	10	11	14	All	
Adult/child	ad	ad	ad	ad	ad	ad	ad	ad	1st chd	2nd Chd
24 Apr-10 May	139	185	195	199	135	155	159	175	39	49
11 May-18 May	157	196	206	213	149	174	178	192	39	49
19 May-25 May	183	222	231	234	176	194	199	209	79	89
26 May-29 May	228	249	257	259	222	241	246	249	99	109
30 May-14 Jun	206	239	249	269	199	232	237	261	89	99
15 Jun-21 Jun	216	259	269	289	204	251	256	282	99	109
22 Jun-5 Jul	234	295	306	337	227	279	284	319	119	139
6 Jul-12 Jul	259	316	326	354	(252)	289	296	324	(129)	(149)
13 Jul-19 Jul	284	338	348	382	276	321	328	362	139	159
20 Jul-7 Aug	319	352	364	397	312	351	359	391	169	199
8 Aug-14 Aug	309	335	345	375	302	344	355	381	169	199
15 Aug-21 Aug	304	324	334	355	297	322	339	360	169	199
22 Aug-28 Aug	274	305	315	339	264	304	309	334	129	139
29 Aug-11 Sep	237	269	279	301	230	269	274	298	119	129
12 Sep-25 Sep	208	234	255	255	211	234	238	252	89	89
26 Sep-9 Oct	180	194	204	204	172	193	197	203	59	59
10 Oct-18 oct	170	179	184	187	164	169	175	181	59	59
19 Oct-28 Oct	190	192	196	–	182	185	185	–	89	89

Dept dates on or during Supplements per adult per night in £:		low	mid	high	low	mid	high
	for 5				0.80	1.00	1.20
	for 4				2.00	2.30	2.90
	for 3	1.90	2.80	2.80	4.30	4.70	5.70
	for 2	5.70	7.30	8.60	8.70	9.60	(11.10)

Season: low 1/4-25/5 & 26/9-5/11; mid 26/5-5/7 & 29/8-25/9; high 6/7-28/8

John's and Susan's holiday costing

Fig. 3. Sample self catering pricing grid.

Note that generally the basic prices in self catering properties are based on the maximum number of adults sharing the property.

Figure 3 shows a sample self catering pricing grid.

COPING WITH THE SUPPLEMENTS

Making sense of flight supplements

After deciding on the day and date of your holiday, you then turn to the back of the brochure. Here the flight timings are listed as well as the flight supplements which need to be added to your basic holiday price.

Why the need for flight supplements?

Tour operators have flight supplements because the basic cost of the holiday is based on flying from Gatwick airport, generally midweek, on a night flight.

● Midweek flights mean departing on Monday, Tuesday, Wednesday or Thursday.

● Weekend flights mean departing on Friday, Saturday or Sunday.

● Day flights depart between 0600 and 2100.

● Night flights depart between 2100 and 0600.

Therefore supplements are added from regional airports and also for better flight timings. Generally the further the airport is from Gatwick the higher the flight supplement.

Night flights are cheaper than day flights and midweek flights are cheaper than weekend flights.

Keeping flight supplements to a minimum

To keep your flight supplements to a minimum, you need to aim at midweek, night flights, which will in theory save you money.

But beware. If you are not arriving back into this country until 0600, that means you will probably not leave your holiday hotel until gone midnight, depending on its proximity to the airport. It is standard practice to vacate rooms by noon on the day of departure. However, many hotels do provide courtesy rooms for changing.

Calculating your flight supplement costs

To calculate your flight supplement:

1. Find the flight chart which applies to your destination – for example, Palma for Majorca.

No of nights	Dept day	Dept time	Return day	Return time	Departures between	6/4- 30/4	1/5- 29/5	30/5- 28/6	29/6- 19/7	20/7- 31/7	1/8- 28/10
Manchester			2 hrs 30 mins								
7/14	Tues	0745	Tues	1330	27 Apr-26 Oct	38	41	46	46	45	45
10	Tues	0745	Thur	2000	27 Apr-19 Oct	33	33	33	30	30	30
7/14	Fri	2330	Sat	0530	28 Apr-20 Oct	23	27	27	24	24	24
11	Fri	0745	Tues	1300	5 May-20 Oct	–	47	48	44	44	44
Birmingham			2 hrs 20 mins								
7/14	Tues	2330	Wed	0535	7 May-22 Oct	–	8	11	11	11	11
7/14	Sun	1415	Sun	2000	7 May-22 Oct	–	55	55	55	55	54
11	Sun	1415	Thur	1330	7 May-22 Oct	–	45	45	45	42	42
Gatwick			2 hrs 5 mins								
7/14	Tues	2350	Wed	0545	7 May-22 Oct	–	0	0	5	14	0
11	Fri	1500	Tues	2020	5 May-20 Oct	–	19	27	34	34	34
7/14	Sun	0725	Sun	1300	5 May-19 Oct	–	25	30	36	36	34

Supplement per person for departing on or between

□ *Flight supplement for Edward's and Jean's holiday*

○ *Flight supplement for Nancy's holiday*

◇ *Flight supplement for John's and Susan's holiday*

Fig. 4. Sample flight chart showing supplements.

2. Decide which regional airport you want to fly from.

3. Choose your departure day.

4. Choose the departure time that best suits you and check the time next to it which tells you when you arrive back in the UK.

5. Look for your departure date at the top right hand side of the chart usually.

6. Where the two lines meet will be your flight supplement.

Remember that these prices are per person and apply to children as well.
    Figure 4 shows a sample flight chart and applicable supplements.

Remembering the extras
You now have a basic price and flight supplement. However, additional supplements can be charged both for hotel and apartment holidays, depending on the facilities or the number of occupants.
    Note that unless otherwise stated these supplements are charged per person per night and not per week or per stay.

Adding the under occupancy charges
Under occupancy charges only apply to self catering holidays, as the basic prices are based on the apartment being fully occupied. For example:

● 4 full fare paying passengers sharing a one bedroomed apartment
● 6 full fare paying passengers sharing a two bedroomed apartment.

So if two people want to share a one bedroomed apartment or similarly if two of the passengers are children and are entitled to a child reduction, then the apartment is under occupied. The same applies if four people wish to share a two bedroomed apartment or if some of the members are children.
    As a result the tour operators charge what are called under occupancy charges. The more the apartment is under occupied, the higher the charges. This is because the tour operators are missing out on a full price being paid, if another person was occupying that property.
    To calculate the under occupancy charges:

1. Look at the supplements charge at the foot of the apartment pricing grid for your chosen property.

2. Determine which season you are departing in (low, mid or high) by your departure date.

3.   The supplement that you will pay is found where the number of adults in your party and season cross.

4.   As the supplement is per person per night it will need to be multiplied by the number of nights you are staying and then by the number of adults, for example £4.70 x 11 x 3.

Figure 3 shows a sample self catering price grid with the under occupancy supplements underneath it.

Children do not count towards the occupancy of the apartment in most cases, so if two adults and two children are occupying a one bedroomed apartment, under occupancy charges will be based on two adults sharing, because the children receive child reductions.

Adding any single room supplements
If a member of your party requires a single room, there is usually a per night supplement to pay. Some hotels make no extra charge and this will be stated usually under a special offer notice next to the description of the hotel.

If you require a single room it is advisable to book early, since many hotels have only perhaps five or six on offer. Despite having to pay a supplement for them, quite often they can be of substandard quality. Although, depending on the season and on how full the hotel is, sometimes one person can be accommodated in a twin room for their sole use.

Adding other room supplements
Many hotels offering sea view rooms will charge a supplement, again per person per night. Very occasionally supplements are charged for rooms with balcony, but this tends to be in older hotels.

Always check the hotel description to ensure that your room contains what you want and that you have not missed any supplements.

Adding any board supplements
Board means the meals included in the basic price. The different types of board are as follows:

● room only – no food included
● self catering – no food included
● bed and breakfast – breakfast only
● half board – breakfast and evening meal
● full board – breakfast, lunch and evening meal.

Extra meals can be requested at the time of booking for a supplement per person per night. If you do not intend having the extra meal every day, it may be better to just pay locally on the days when it is required. Quite often the hotel restaurants are open to the public as well as to residents, which makes this possible. If half board is included in your basic price and you wish to book full board, but do not want to be tied to returning to the hotel for lunch, quite often they will furnish you with a packed lunch instead.

Many hotels now have buffet style meals even at breakfast. If this does not suit you, check the hotel description for one offering waiter service.

In Spain, Italy, Tunisia and Malta the hotels tend to be based on half board with full board available at a supplement. In Turkey, Greece and Portugal, the majority is based on bed and breakfast with half board available at a supplement. Most destinations have self catering accommodation.

Aparthotels
You will see that some properties in the brochures are classed as **aparthotels**. This means that they are priced as apartments and are based on self catering, so no meals are included, but there is a half board option which is usually listed under the occupancy charges. Again this option is charged per person per night.

Deducting the room reductions

There are reductions in some hotels if three or four adults share a room, as the room can become more cramped than if two adults and two children shared it. Therefore if this applies to your chosen hotel, a per person per night reduction will be listed on the pricing grid. It is known as a 3rd/4th adult sharing reduction.

INFANT AND CHILD PRICES: QUESTIONS AND ANSWERS

Who are classed as infants?
Children under two years of age on the return date of travel.

How much does it cost to take an infant on holiday?
The fee varies among tour operators, but it is generally about £19.

Are there any extra costs connected with infants?
No deposit is payable for an infant, but any food purchased or cot provided for them should be paid for direct to the hotel. Make sure the room is large enough to accommodate a cot.

Do infants have a seat of their own?
No, as they only pay a nominal charge a seat is not allocated to them, and they must sit on an adult's lap for take off and landing. If there are vacant seats, then the infant can use one during the flight.

Do infants have their own baggage allowance?
No, but a folding pushchair will be carried free of charge.

What happens if children are passed off as infants?
The appropriate price will be charged for the child before boarding a plane.
If sufficient seats are not available as a result, permission to board the plane
will be refused as airline regulations state that children must have a seat of
their own.

What conditions are attached to free child places?
Generally speaking the age limit is 11 years inclusive in hotels and 16 years
inclusive in apartments, but check with the individual tour operator. The
child must share the room with two adults and the ages of the children must
be stated on the booking form at the time of booking.

Are there any extra costs connected with free child places?
Yes, a deposit is still payable but will be deducted from the holiday balance.
The usual supplements still have to be paid as does the insurance for that
child.

Do free child places save money?
Not always, even with a free child place sometimes the same or similar
holiday with a different tour operator could work out cheaper. Thorough
investigations prior to booking are essential in order to receive the best
deal.

What reductions will there be if all free child places have gone?
When this happens the first child price shown on the pricing grid in Figure
1 applies. The second child usually receives a set amount off the adult price
shown in the price panel.

What is topping and tailing?
This is the term applied when two children share a bed, instead of occupying separate ones, to save space in the hotel room.

Is there an age limit on topping and tailing?
Yes, two children may share a bed provided that their combined ages do not
total more than ten years.

REMEMBERING TO ADD INSURANCE COSTS

Insurance premiums need to be added when costing the holiday, but
insurance is discussed in depth in Chapter 4.

Figure 5 shows typical insurance premiums which have been used for the costings in this chapter.

Length of stay	Adults	Child	Family
Up to 8 days	20.50	8.75	47.65
Up to 15 days	25.50	12.75	67.75
Infants – no charge			
Child up to 16 years inclusive			
Family – 2 adults and 4 children			

Fig. 5. Typical insurance premiums

UNDERSTANDING THE PRICE VARIATIONS

You will notice that the brochure prices are considerably lower from the end of April to the start of June. The reduced prices reflect the unpredictable nature of the weather at this time of year.

If you want to avoid the scorching sun and not feel like a sardine in busy resorts, then early season might be the best time for you to travel and save money.

Being aware of the disadvantages

Since most people who holiday abroad are seeking uninterrupted sunshine, the numbers of holidaymakers travelling early season are considerably lower than later in the season. This can lead to the following problems:

- tour operators tend to merge two flights into one, which could mean different flight timings from what you originally booked, or even a different day of travel

- hotel changes are not uncommon if there are insufficient bookings

- facilities at some hotels and apartments can be limited if numbers are low

- hotels which are only half full sometimes lack the atmosphere created in high season

- in early season some of the resort's shops, bars and restaurants are closed, again leading to a lack of atmosphere

CHECKLIST

Arriving at the correct hotel cost

Hotels

- Have you arrived at the correct basic cost?
- Have you added the appropriate flight supplement?
- Have you added any necessary single room supplements?
- Have you added any relevant room supplements?
- Have you added any extra board supplements?
- Have you deducted any applicable room reductions?
- Have you calculated the child prices correctly?
- Have you added any applicable infant charges?
- Have you added the insurance premiums?

Arriving at the correct self catering cost

Self-catering

- Have you arrived at the correct basic cost?
- Have you added the appropriate flight supplement?
- Have you added the relevant under occupancy charges?
- Have you added any extra board supplements if in aparthotel?
- Have you calculated the child prices correctly?
- Have you added any applicable infant charges?
- Have you added the insurance premiums?

CASE STUDIES

Edward's and Jean's hotel costing

Edward and Jean have decided to opt for an 11 night holiday. As they are both retired they are not restricted to weekend travel, and want a civilised day flight from Manchester: they do not mind paying a higher flight supplement to obtain good timings. They also want a sea view room. They want to be away for their wedding anniversary on 16 May.

The costing for their holiday is based on the hotel pricing grid in Figure 1 and the flight chart and supplements in Figure 4:

2 adults for 11 nights on Friday 12 May @ £376.00	=	£752.00
2 flight supplements from Manchester @ £47.00	=	£94.00
2 sea view supplements @ £3.60 each x 11 nights	=	£79.20
2 adult insurances @ £25.50	=	£51.00
Total holiday cost	=	£976.20

Nancy's hotel costing

Nancy has decided to go away for two weeks and will need a single room since she is travelling alone. Due to other commitments she wants to travel after 19 September and needs a weekend departure. She does not want to travel late at night, and her nearest departure airport is Birmingham. She would prefer to stay in the hotel complex for meals and so requires full board.

The costing for her holiday based on the hotel pricing grid in Figure 1 and the flight chart and supplements in Figure 4 will be as follows:

1 adult for 14 nights on Sunday 21 September @ £549.00	£549.00
1 flight supplement from Birmingham @ £54.00	£54.00
1 single room supplement @ £8.10 x 14 nights	£113.40
1 full board supplement @ £ 5.15 x 14 nights	£72.10
1 adult insurance @ £25.50	£25.50
Total holiday cost	£814.00

John's and Susan's apartment costing

John and Susan need to travel as cheaply as possible, so are opting for an apartment holiday for one week only. To keep costs low they are prepared to travel on night flights and can go midweek, but cannot travel before 6 July in order to fit in with school holidays. Having two children and a baby with them, the have decided on a two bedroomed apartment instead of a one bedroomed to give them more room and privacy, even though it will be more expensive. Their local airport is Gatwick. They have left it too late to obtain a free child place.

The costing for their holiday based on the apartment pricing grid in Figure 3 and the flight chart and supplements in Figure 4 will be as follows:

2 adults for 7 nights on Tuesday 10 July @ £252.00	£504.00
1 child price @ £129.00	£129.00
2nd child price @ £149.00	£149.00
Infant cost @ £15.00	£15.00
4 flight supplements from Gatwick @ £5.00	£20.00
2 under occupancy supplements @ £11.10 x 7 nights	£155.40
Family insurance @ £47.65	£47.65
Total holiday cost	£1020.05

In reality all the people in the case studies would not book at the same hotel as they all have different requirements from a holiday, as is made clear later. The pricing grids have been applied to each set of people purely to demonstrate how to cost the holiday.

DISCUSSION POINTS

1. When costing your holiday before reading this chapter, which elements did you find confusing or forget to include?

2. What would you do to make the brochures easier to understand?

3. How much is your holiday going to cost? Have you compared several tour operators' brochures who feature you choice of hotel/apartment, to ensure you are getting the best price?

2
Choosing the Right Destination

ASSESSING YOUR PRIORITIES

When choosing a holiday destination, many people simply glance through the brochures and see which destination looks the most appealing from the photographs of sandy beaches, shimmering seas and fabulous hotels. However, in reality, the destination is the most important choice you will have to make. That choice will probably determine the success of your holiday.

The best way to choose the right destination is to sort out what your priorities are, and make sure that everyone agrees on them. Having established what your criteria are, you can then begin scouring the brochures.

It is pointless to pick a destination out of the brochure because of its safe sandy beaches and crystal clear waters, when the children are too old to play on a beach and the adults would sooner be around the pool, and no one is interested in venturing into the sea.

Determining your holiday type

The destination is largely determined by the type of holiday you are seeking. Whilst those with a passion for sightseeing would be bored to tears on a beach for two weeks, similarly those seeking non stop action day and night would detest a holiday in a remote Alpine village.

It is therefore important to take time to match up your preferred style of holiday with what the resorts have to offer. This is a lot easier than it sounds because many of the tour operators – for example, Thomsons – categorise their resorts into holiday types by means of a symbol. Others print the information at the start of each resort section highlighting certain resorts for the different types of holiday.

Questions and answers

Where can I find a relaxing holiday?
The quieter and more peaceful resorts include Funchal in Madeira, Los Gigantes in Tenerife, Mellieha Bay in Malta and the Canary Island of Fuerteventura.

Which resorts are scenic?
Picture-postcard towns and villages set amongst beautiful scenery include Sorrento, Amalfi and Maiori in Italy, resorts in northern Majorca and northern Ibiza and Funchal in Madeira.

Where can I go for plenty of sightseeing?
For those who want to explore wrecks and ruins and resorts steeped in history try Sorrento in Italy, Hammamet in Tunisia, Paphos in Cyprus, Kusadasi and Side in Turkey. Malta and Egypt have many resorts where sightseeing is plentiful.

Excellent beaches are important to me, where can I find them?
The most beautiful beaches suitable for the sun worshipper and swimmer alike can be found in Ayia Napa in Cyprus, Puerto Pollensa in Majorca. Most resorts in Tunisia, Fuerteventura in the Canary Islands and resorts on the Adriatic and Venetian Rivieras in Italy offer excellent beaches.

Which resorts cater especially for families?
Family resorts cater for all the family including children of all ages and include Praia da Rocha in the Algarve, Lido Di Jesolo in Italy, Protaras in Cyprus and Mojacar on the Costa de Almeria. Numerous resorts in Majorca and the majority in Minorca are also geared up for families.

Lively resorts, where are they?
These resorts are buzzing with bars, discos and nightclubs with plenty to do day and night. Resorts include Palma Nova/Magalluf in Majorca, San Antonio in Ibiza, Torremolinos on the Costa del Sol, Benidorm, Lloret, Salou, Playa de las Americas in Tenerife, Playa del Ingles in Gran Canaria and Ayia Napa in Cyprus.

Where can I find plenty of sports?
Sports including tennis, water skiing, windsurfing, diving, horse riding and so on can be found in the following resorts: Protaras in Cyprus, the majority of resorts in Gran Canaria and Majorca and Malta. Different sports can be found in other resorts, but it is advisable to check first.

Which resorts cater for golfers?
Resorts with excellent golf facilities nearby include Algarve, Costa del Sol, and Costa Blanca.

Where can I take a two centre holiday?
These holidays are ideal for people who want to visit two resorts in one holiday. Resorts which can be combined include Costa del Sol and Gibraltar,

Costa de la Luz and Gibraltar, Greece and Turkey, two different resorts in Turkey, Rome and Sorrento, Lake Garda and Lido di Jesolo in Italy, mainland Greece and the Greek island of Poros,

Where can I go for a two island holiday?
Add variety to your holiday by dividing your stay between two different islands. Combinations include Malta and Gozo, Tenerife and Gran Canaria, Tenerife and Lanzarote, Lanzarote and Fuerteventura, Tenerife and Fuerteventura.

Where do cruising holidays go?
Holidays are available for pure cruising or on a cruise-and-stay basis, where some time is spent in a hotel in one of the resorts. Options include cruise to Egypt and Israel then stay in Cyprus, complete cruise on the Nile, cruise to Greek islands and Turkey then stay in Greece, cruise to Greek islands then stay in Cyprus, cruise around the Mediterranean and stay in Lake Garda or Lido di Jesolo in Italy.

Where can I visit on a touring holiday?
Some tours can be combined with a week in a beach resort. Touring holidays are not really suitable for young children, and a holiday which is nothing but touring can be very tiring. Combinations available include tour around Andalusia and stay on Costa del Sol, tour Portugal and stay on Portuguese Algarve, tour Bulgaria and Istanbul and stay in a Black Sea resort, tour Turkey and stay in Turkish beach resort, complete tours of Italy, Sicily and Greece, tour Italy and stay in Sorrento, tour Greece and stay on Greek island of Poros.

What is an all inclusive holiday and where can I take one?
An all inclusive holiday is one where all your food and drink and some activities are included in the cost. If you eat and drink a lot and enjoy plenty of activities and sports then they are good value for money. It is important to check what is actually included since it does vary from resort to resort. There are different types of all inclusive holidays on offer: some for adults only, some for families and some which are not geared to any particular group. Destinations include Costa Blanca, Costa del Sol, Greek island of Evia, Majorca, Minorca, Ibiza, Lanzarote, Fuerteventura, Malta, Cyprus, Rhodes, Crete and Turkey.

USING YOUR TRAVEL AGENT

If you cannot find out all the answers to your queries from the brochures, do not be afraid to quiz your travel agent. That is what he is there for.

Finding out the truth

It is important to remember when looking at the holiday brochures that they are primarily trying to sell you something. Some of the unpleasant features of a holiday resort, such as busy railway lines, shanty towns, beggars and waste sites, will almost certainly not be mentioned.

It is important to know the full facts about your chosen resort. Do not hesitate to ask your travel agent if you can read the resort write-up in the *Agents Hotel Gazeteer*.

This reference book not only provides unbiased information on numerous hotels and apartments abroad, but also on the holiday resorts themselves. Maps of the resorts show what facilities are available, including the type of beach and how many discos, restaurants, bars and so on there are. Medical facilities and chemist are also listed.

Nothing is hidden from the holidaymaker in this non glossy book, which is not trying to sell you anything, unlike the brochures. It is known in the travel trade as the truth book.

Building in the resort

Travel agents also have computerised access to building work information in resorts. Once you have a resort in mind, ask your travel agent to check:

● any building programmes in progress and when they are due to be completed
● any building programmes planned, and when
● what degree of disruption any work is likely to cause.

Building work is assessed on a scale depending upon its severity and the disruption it is expected to cause. All the information on the computer is updated on a regular basis by the tour operators.

As building work can make such a big difference to a resort, it is advisable to investigate before booking your holiday.

Obtaining further information

If you require further information on holiday resorts, it may be a good idea to contact the relevant tourist information offices. You will find a list of the popular destinations' tourist offices in the Useful Addresses section. If the country which you require is not listed, your travel agent should be able to find out the relevant information.

Using the library

The library is a good source of extra information, since they do stock a large number of travel guides on both popular and unusual destinations.

The more information and facts you can mass on a destination, the more in the picture you will feel.

ASSESSING FLIGHT AND TRANSFER LENGTHS

For people who are not keen on flying or do not like long coach journeys, especially with children, flight and transfer lengths are important facts to consider when choosing a holiday destination.

Before you book, make sure you are aware of:

- the length of the flight to your chosen destination
- the length of the coach transfer to your chosen resort from the airport.

Figure 6 shows the approximate flight lengths to the popular package holiday destinations in Europe, based on departing from London. Add an extra 30 minutes for departures from Scottish airports. If you are considering a destination further afield, beware, the flight lengths are considerably longer, and often travel through the night.

Figure 7 shows which resorts are more than two hours by coach from the airport.

CONSIDERING OTHER FACTORS

There are further factors to consider when travelling abroad, especially if it is your first time. Different people attach greater importance to different aspects of their holiday.

Weighing up the weather

The weather can be an important consideration for some people, as far as exposure to the sun is concerned. Those who burn easily will be more comfortable travelling early or late season, *ie* April/May or late September/ October.

However, the holiday season is short in some resorts due to the weather changing later in the year. This is particularly true of Corfu, where it rains heavily from mid September onwards. This fact is reflected in the prices for holidays there which plummet from mid September onwards. Many other resorts become unsettled and have mixed weather from mid September, quite often accompanied by thunderstorms. However, in the Canary Islands the temperatures vary only a few degrees throughout the year, and therefore nothing is gained or lost by visiting early or late.

Avoiding intense heat
The resorts to avoid due to the intense heat during the months of July and August are:

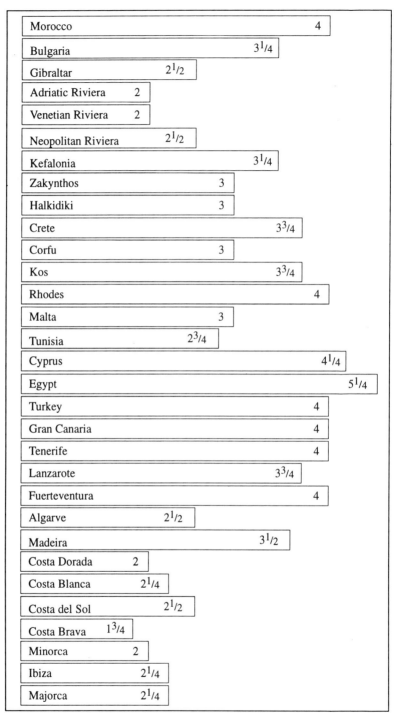

Fig. 6. Approximate flight lengths in hours to popular destinations.

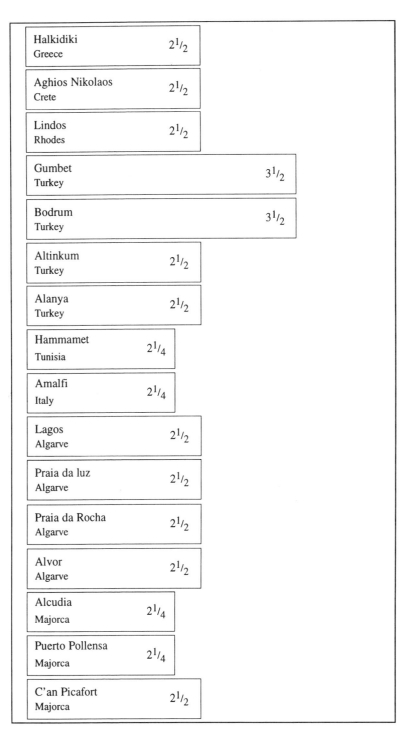

Resort	Country	Hours
Halkidiki	Greece	$2^1/_2$
Aghios Nikolaos	Crete	$2^1/_2$
Lindos	Rhodes	$2^1/_2$
Gumbet	Turkey	$3^1/_2$
Bodrum	Turkey	$3^1/_2$
Altinkum	Turkey	$2^1/_2$
Alanya	Turkey	$2^1/_2$
Hammamet	Tunisia	$2^1/_4$
Amalfi	Italy	$2^1/_4$
Lagos	Algarve	$2^1/_2$
Praia da luz	Algarve	$2^1/_2$
Praia da Rocha	Algarve	$2^1/_2$
Alvor	Algarve	$2^1/_2$
Alcudia	Majorca	$2^1/_4$
Puerto Pollensa	Majorca	$2^1/_4$
C'an Picafort	Majorca	$2^1/_2$

Fig. 7. Resort transfers over two hours by coach.

- Greek Islands
- Cyprus
- Turkey
- Egypt

However, it must be said that most of the European package holiday resorts exceed 27°C/80°F at this time of year.

Do not forget that the sun is at its hottest and strongest between twelve noon and 1500 hrs. If you can avoid being in it between these times, you will not find the heat quite as unbearable.

Studying the temperatures
In most holiday brochures you will find a temperature chart for each destination: usually at the start of each destination with other resort information. Figure 8 shows a temperature chart for Majorca. As you can see it gives the average daily temperature for London and Majorca, along with the average daily hours of sunshine in Majorca.

If this sort of information does not appear in your chosen holiday brochures, again ask your travel agent.

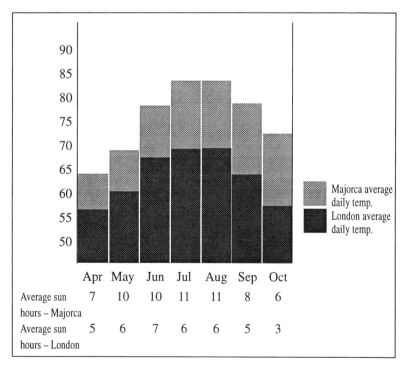

	Apr	May	Jun	Jul	Aug	Sep	Oct
Average sun hours – Majorca	7	10	10	11	11	8	6
Average sun hours – London	5	6	7	6	6	5	3

Fig. 8. Sample temperature/sunshine chart for Majorca.

Accepting the language barrier

In the majority of holiday resorts some English is spoken, but it isn't always the case. Sometimes it can be difficult making yourself understood. If you do not want to encounter such problems you would probably be better visiting:

- Malta
- Gibraltar
- Cyprus.

Spain does not usually present too many problems but Turkey, Greece and North Africa can be another story. However, your holiday representative, who will speak the local language fluently, is on hand to help out if necessary.

Making the effort

It can pay to learn a few simple phrases in the local language, since most of the locals are very pleased if you make an effort. The words please, thank you, Good morning, how are you and so on are sufficient. You will be amazed by the response you receive as a result of trying. Simple phrase books are widely available in shops and libraries.

PRICING THE COST OF LIVING ABROAD

Pricing what things cost whilst you are on holiday may sound miserly, but it can make the difference between a cheap and a very expensive holiday.

Some tour operators display typical costs at the start of each resort in the brochure, to give the holidaymaker an idea of the cost of eating out, and everyday expenditure on holiday.

Being aware of sudden changes

Sweeping price changes can occur suddenly due to strengths and weaknesses of currencies. This can result in what was a cheap destination turning into an expensive one.

The cheaper resorts at present for British holidaymakers include:

- Spain
- Bulgaria
- Turkey
- Greece.

The more expensive ones include:

- France
- Austria
- Cyprus.

Do check with your travel agent, who should be able to advise you if fluctuating exchange rates have resulted in a resort becoming a lot cheaper, or a lot more expensive.

Keeping expenditure down

When eating out always opt for restaurants off the tourist trail, where the locals eat. Not only will it be cheaper but the standard of food is generally higher as well. If your holiday representative recommends a restaurant the chances are they receive commission for doing so.

Certain everyday items in the resorts can be very expensive, such as tea bags, coffee, English brands of tinned food, cereals, nappies and so on. If they are essential to you, save money by taking them with you. Exploring the local markets is a cheap way to shop and adds new experiences to your holiday.

TRAVELLING WITH THE DISABLED

If there are physically disabled people in your party, then it is essential that you check the geography of your proposed resort with your travel agent. They have access to information on the accessibility of resorts, some of which are set in very steep terrain.

This will inevitably reduce the number of destinations open to you, but it is far better to find out before you travel that a place is neither practical nor suitable for your needs.

Taking wheelchairs

For people in wheelchairs, travel agents have information on accommodation accessibility including hotel room and dining room dimensions, number of steps to the pool area, lift accesses and so on. They can advise you about plane accessibility and taking your own wheelchair.

ACCEPTING RECOMMENDATIONS FROM FRIENDS

Resort recommendations from friends or relatives should be investigated thoroughly. They will return from their holiday bubbling with enthusiasm and armed with photographs, but would they really admit it if it had been a total disaster?

Their requirements are not necessarily your requirements. If after careful consideration you find that the recommended resort would suit your family, then by all means find as much information out from them as possible, since personal information can be very valuable.

Seeking information from them

Information on the best excursions to take, and whether it is cheaper and better to organise them yourself or go through the holiday representative, is usually invaluable.

If you intend travelling during the same season as the people who have already travelled, tips on good local restaurants and bars to visit will be useful. However, by the following year the establishment may have changed management.

CHECKLIST

- Have you considered your holiday priorities?
- Have you decided what your holiday type is?
- Do you have all the information you need?
- Have you consulted the *Agents Hotel Gazateer*?
- Have you considered the flight and transfer lengths?
- Is the weather an important factor?
- Does the language barrier bother you?
- Have you considered the cost of living abroad?
- Do you have disabled people travelling?

CASE STUDIES

Edward and Jean choose Turkey

Edward and Jean like to obtain as much information about their chosen resort as possible. They do not hesitate to quiz their travel agent in order to find out what the resorts are really like, and borrow library books to give them extra information.

They like to go off exploring, but they do need a resort which is not too hilly because of Jean's angina.

Flight and transfer lengths hold no importance to them as they are keen to see as much of the country they are visiting as possible. Being retired, they tend to travel early or late season so weather does not bother them. They are keen to learn a little of the local language and enjoy experimenting with it. Money is not a problem so the cost of living abroad does not really matter.

After studying endless brochures they finally decide to go to Side in Turkey mainly because of the abundance of sightseeing.

Nancy plumps for Crete

Nancy is not a lover of brochures, claiming the more she looks at the more confused she becomes. However, she knows what her preferences are and is prepared to discuss them with her travel agent, in order to find the right destination.

She wants a relaxing holiday in a relatively inexpensive resort which has excellent beaches and tennis facilities. She does not intend venturing out at night and so isn't interested in a lively resort. Nancy needs to travel late season and is a sun worshipper, so it needs to be hot and sunny in September and October.

After lengthy discussion with the travel agent, Nancy accepts the suggestion of a holiday in Georgioupolis on Crete.

John and Susan decide on Majorca

John and Susan have never been abroad before and so need all the advice they can get. However, they are not really interested in listening to information, with the exception of some given by their friends who had a fabulous time in Magalluf in Majorca two years ago, but they had no children.

As John and Susan have three children they need a wide range of facilities and a short flight and transfer time. They need to travel in school holidays and one child is sensitive to the sun. Their limited finances demand a resort which is not going to be very expensive.

Since their friends suggested Magalluf, John and Susan have decided that this is the resort for them. Whilst Majorca is a good choice for first time travellers, this young and lively resort is not over suited to families. Nevertheless, it appears that nothing will change their minds.

DISCUSSION POINTS

1. Which of the three case studies most reflects your own position?

2. What do you consider to be the three most important factors when choosing your holiday destination?

3. Do you think the tour operators provide enough information in their brochures. What would you like to see covered which isn't already featured?

3
Selecting Accommodation

DEFINING THE DIFFERENT TYPES

Accommodation abroad is split into two main groups:

● hotel rooms
● apartments.

What will my hotel room consist of?

Generally a hotel room contains one to four beds depending on how many people it is accommodating. The third and fourth beds often fold away. Most hotel rooms have a separate bathroom with WC, bath and/or shower. There is usually wardrobe and drawer storage space. If there are more than two people sharing the room, storage space can be limited.

Most hotel rooms include a balcony in the cost; however in older hotels you may have to pay a supplement. Often there are a couple of chairs and a table on the balcony.

Some of the expensive hotels often provide a mini mar. This small fridge contains miniatures of spirits, beer and mixers which are charged for at a grossly inflated rate. There is no room in the fridge to store drinks bought outside the hotel.

Hotels provide bed linen and towels, although towels are not be taken out of the room. Take your own for the beach. Beds are made daily.

What can I expect in my apartment?

The sleeping arrangements in an apartment are determined by its size and the number of occupants. If the apartment is occupied to capacity, some people have to sleep in the lounge area. The arrangements are generally as follows:

● In studios which take two or three people, all members sleep in the living area as there arc no separate bedrooms.

● In one bedroomed apartments occupied by two people, they can sleep in the separate bedroom.

- In one bedroomed apartments occupied by three or four people, two sleep in the bedroom and two in the lounge area.

- In two bedroomed apartments occupied by four people, each of the two bedrooms accommodate two people.

- In two bedroomed apartments occupied by six people, the extra two have to sleep in the lounge area, with the other four in the two bedrooms.

The beds in the lounge area of studios and apartments are in the form of bed setees, so that there is seating space during the day. Table and chairs can be found here and possibly a television.

In all types of studio and apartment a separate bathroom is provided containing a WC, bath and/or shower.

The kitchen area is usually within the lounge space. Generally the kitchen contains a fridge, gas/electric rings, grill, sometimes a small oven and sink. There are basic cooking utensils, cutlery and pots and pans. Do not expect to be able to cook a three course meal: snacks and light meals would be more realistic.

Bed linen is provided and is usually changed at least each week. Sometimes towels are provided but generally not. The occupants are expected to make their beds and clean the apartment.

Private individual villas
There are specialist brochures which feature private individual villas. Each villa, usually with its own grounds and private pool, is separate, spacious and quite luxurious. Some can be quite isolated and car hire is essential. Many have microwaves, satellite television, videos and freezers – which is reflected in the price. Tour operators which feature this type of holiday include Meon Villas, Beach Villas and Sunworld holidays.

CONSIDERING THE LOCATION AND FACILITIES

There are many factors to consider when choosing both hotels or apartments, according to your circumstances and personal requirements.

Discovering the truth about the location
While the description in the holiday brochure may sound ideal, beware – it could turn out to be quite the opposite. As the brochure is trying to sell you a holiday, certain local undesirable factors may have been omitted from the description.

In order to get a true picture of where the property is located, be certain to ask your travel agent to let you see the property in the *Agents Hotel Gazeteer*. This will provide you with unbiased information including:

- a map showing your chosen property's proximity to the sea, beaches, bars and restaurants

- any undesirable objects nearby such as noisy railway lines, bus stations, busy roads, smelly rivers or harbours and so on

- whether the nearby beach is of shingle, rock or soft white sand.

- whether your chosen property is on the flat or if you have to hike up and down a mountainous road.

Discovering the truth about the facilities

Again descriptions on the hotel or apartment facilities may not be totally truthful; certain facts may be omitted altogether.

Do not hesitate to look up the property in the *Agents Hotel Gazeteer* which will advise you:

- if there are enough lifts, to avoid having to wait every time you leave your room

- if the pool and number of sunloungers are adequate for the number of residents

- if the restaurant is in the main building or in an annexe or shared with another property.

Studying different brochures

When you see a property that you like, check several brochures to see if it is featured in them. Sometimes photographs taken from different angles can give you a totally different impression. The hotel or apartment descriptions can vary among the tour operators, each one concentrating on various aspects of the property.

Matching your requirements to what is on offer

You will have to decide whether the facilities offered at your chosen property suit your particular requirements by considering the following:

- the size of the hotel or apartment complex
- the type and frequency of entertainments

- the facilities available for children
- whether the property is geared towards families
- the type of restaurant: buffet style or waiter service
- the sports facilities
- whether the property is air conditioned
- if self catering, whether there is a supermarket on the complex.

By matching your requirements with the facilities on offer at your hotel or apartment, you should avoid choosing a property that is just not geared to your needs.

UNDERSTANDING ACCOMMODATION RATINGS

As you browse through the brochures you will notice various systems of rating hotels and apartments. Some have different letters such as 'A,T,S' and some use symbols such as diamonds and asterisks.

You will also notice that each property has two ratings. One given by the tour operator, which is normally found under the property name, and one at the end of the property description which is the official rating.

You probably find this all very confusing, so the Question and Answer section below explains the systems.

Questions and answers

What is an official rating?
This is the rating given by the tourist authority of the individual countries.

Why are stars, keys and letters given for official ratings?
In Spain and its islands, Portugal, Italy, Malta, Cyprus, Turkey, Tunisia and Morocco they generally use a star system for hotels and a key system for apartments. However, in Malta and Cyprus they use a letter system for apartments. In Greece and its islands they use a mixture of systems for hotels and apartments.

Why do tour operators have their own rating systems?
This is because different countries use different official systems which create confusion.

How do the tour operator's ratings work?
The tour operator will award either a letter or symbol to each property whether hotel or apartment according to its food, facilities, location, service and so on, on a scale of one (basic) to five (luxury).

ASSESSING THE PROS AND CONS

Advantages

There are advantages to staying in either a hotel or an apartment. The decision ultimately is a matter of personal choice and circumstances.

Opting for a hotel
The main reasons why people choose to stay in a hotel are:

● meals are provided, so you do not have to go looking for somewhere to eat every night or cook your own

● children are well catered for in family type hotels, often with early suppers provided

● many hotels now have self service restaurants, so you are free to eat as little or as much as you want

● many hotels cater for English tastes but have foreign dishes as well

● you are generally waited on, with beds made each day and your room tidied and cleaned

● hotels have flexible meal times so you are not too restricted if you are going out during the day

● entertainment is provided day and night for adults and children, depending on the hotel type

● often the holiday representative visits most days, so any problems can be sorted out with the hotel management

● hotels offer a better chance of meeting people if you are travelling alone or have children who want to play with other children

● many hotels organise children's activities to give parents a break.

Opting for an apartment
Some people, especially women, think that an apartment means cooking, shopping and cleaning, and so it is not really much of a holiday. However, this doesn't have to be the case, and many people choose an apartment holiday because of the following factors:

● apartments are more spacious than hotel rooms, especially if you are travelling with children

- you have more freedom: you can get up when you like, eat when you want, and what you like at mealtimes

- you can eat in or out, and choose a different restaurant every night of you wish

- there is not usually as much entertainment at night in apartments, so it is quieter for sleeping especially if you have young children

- child reductions – especially for older children – are generally greater in apartments

- there are facilities for making tea and coffee and snacks

- a fridge is provided, so drinks can be kept cool

- apartments offer more privacy: children can have their own room.

Disadvantages

As there are disadvantages to most things, it is important to be aware of them when deciding which type of accommodation to opt for.

Not staying in hotels

The factors which discourage people from staying in an hotel are:

- there isn't as much freedom in hotels due to meals and the maid coming in to clean your room

- there is no fridge to store your drinks in, so you have to buy from the hotel bar which is expensive, or buy them from the supermarket but drink them warm

- there are no facilities for making tea or coffee during the day so again you have to buy it

- if you do not like the food in the hotel you are stuck with it for the length of your stay

- if you have young children who go to bed early, the hotel room isn't very comfortable for sitting in

- rooms can be cramped especially if you are sharing it with children, and there isn't much privacy.

Not staying in an apartment
The reasons for not staying in an apartment are:

● you are responsible for keeping your apartment clean, washing up and so on

● a deposit in local currency is payable on some apartments on arrival, to insure against damage or breakages (it is refunded if there is no damage)

● there are not as many activities available, and it is more difficult to meet other people

● upstairs apartments are not always served by a lift, which could present problems for the elderly or people with prams

● quite often the apartment owner does not live at the apartments, and so sorting out complaints can be a problem

● the holiday representative may not make as many visits to apartments as to hotels

● if you do eat out every day it can be expensive and needs to be budgeted for.

Determining the type of accommodation by destination

In some cases your destination will determine whether you stay in an apartment or in an hotel.

This is particularly true of the North African resorts such as Tunisia and Morocco. In these resorts self catering is not really recommended, especially for all female parties, as it is not safe to go out at night. During the day it is not unusual to experience pestering, begging and mugging by the locals. Because of this the hotels are on complexes where everything is provided including restaurants, bars, discos and entertainment.

In other resorts self catering or bed and breakfast is a must. This is particularly true of the Greek destinations and some of the Turkish ones. Eating out is very reasonably priced and the choice of food is excellent. Generally the hotel food is not as good or as imaginative as the local food. Both Greece and Turkey are very safe for going out during the day and at night.

CHECKLIST

● Do you know what facilities your accommodation has?

- Do you know where exactly your accommodation is situated?
- Do the facilities on offer suit your needs?
- Do you know what rating the accommodation has?
- Have you assessed the advantages of your accommodation type?
- Have you considered the disadvantages of your choice?
- Is your choice determined by destination?

CASE STUDIES

Edward's and Jean's hotel

Edward and Jean are as meticulous about choosing their accommodation as their resort.

They always stay in hotels because they like to be waited on and always select one of the higher class ones which is not geared towards children. They are not bothered about plenty of entertainment and prefer to go for a stroll in the evenings.

Once they have selected a few suitable hotels, and seen photos and descriptions of them in various brochures, they ask the travel agent to look their choices up in the *Agents Hotel Gazeteer* for an unbiased and truthful description. With this information they then make their final choice – a four start hotel in Side in Turkey.

Nancy goes 'all inclusive'

As Nancy is travelling alone, self catering is not really an option for her as even studio accommodation normally does not take just one person.

She discusses her options with the travel agent, who points out the cost benefits of going on an all inclusive holiday: Nancy would know exactly how much she was spending, since most things you require on holiday are included in the price. She is keen on playing tennis and other sports which are included, and plans to spend most of her time relaxing on the hotel complex, so using the facilities to the maximum.

Nancy books the travel agent's suggestion of an all inclusive three star hotel on the beach in Georgioupolis on Crete, which has plenty of entertainment and sports included.

John and Susan want self catering

John is the decision maker and Susan just agrees with him. They decide on self catering in Magalluf, because of a friend's recommendation, and they think it will be cheap. They then go to every local travel agent in search of a holiday.

John wants a free child place for one of the children but is not very pleased when he is told that there is none left. As they are travelling in school holidays and they have left it late for booking, his chances were very slim anyway. One travel agent offers him two sizeable reductions for each of the elder children, self catering in Magalluf, but John decides to wait for a special offer and save more money.

He is advised by several travel agents that the child reductions would probably be cheaper than a special offer, but John will not change his mind.

DISCUSSION POINTS

1. What have John and Susan done wrong? What would you do in their situation and why?

2. Do you find the hotel/apartment rating systems confusing? How would you improve them?

3. Do you think that the tour operators should be more truthful about their hotel and apartment descriptions?

4. Which other information would you like to see displayed in the property descriptions?

4
Knowing about Insurance

Insurance is absolutely essential when travelling abroad, mainly for:

- medical cover
- cancellation cover.

It is a sad fact of life that you don't realise how important insurance is until you have to claim. Many people see it as yet another expense to add to the holiday total, and 20 per cent of people travelling abroad do not take out any insurance.

UNDERSTANDING THE COVER

It is important that you understand exactly what you are covered for when taking out holiday insurance. If you do not understand make sure you ask the travel agent.

The Question and Answer section below covers the basics which most insurance companies cover you for.

How much is my personal baggage covered for?
The insurance covers you for loss or damage of your personal belongings on holiday generally up to £1500, but any one item is limited to £200 in value. So if you are taking an expensive item abroad – for example, a video camera – which exceeds this limit, you may have to cover it separately on your home insurance. Do ensure that it is covered as insurance companies do stick to the levels of cover.

What about my money?
The personal money section of the policy covers you for loss of travellers cheques and foreign currency/cash up to £500. However, there is a limit on cash losses of between £250 and £300 depending on the insurance company. Travellers cheques are insured when you purchase them anyway. If they are lost or stolen a full refund is made through the cheque-issuing company. It is important to limit the amount of cash/currency you exchange at any given time, because of the limit of cover with the insurance.

Are medical and emergency costs covered?
Yes. You are covered if you are injured or need medical treatment whilst abroad. The cover varies from £2,000,000 to £10,000,000 per person depending on the insurance company. Be sure that there is a telephone number for the 24-hour emergency service on the insurance policy, so that if your medical expenses are very expensive, bills can be settled direct through the insurance company. It is important to take the insurance policy on holiday with you as some medical treatment will not be given otherwise. Most insurance companies also cover for extra accommodation expenses and return travel due to illness or injury. Some pay for being a hospital inpatient at a set amount each day up to a maximum. In case of death, most pay for the carriage of the insured person's body back to the UK, or for funeral expenses in the locality of their death.

Am I covered if I have to cancel my holiday?
Yes, you are covered if you have to cancel or curtail your holiday due to injury, illness, death of a relative, jury service and so on – in other words a valid reason for not travelling. Some cover for redundancy or severe damage to your home. The cover is usually up to the final invoice total of the holiday.

What if I have an accident on holiday?
You are covered for death, loss of limbs, eyes or permanent total disablement as the result of an accident. The amount of cover varies from £15,000 to £25,000 per person. Some insurance companies pay reduced benefits to people under 16 or over 76.

What is personal liability?
This covers you for legal liability for accidentally injuring someone or damaging property not belonging to you. The cover varies from £1,000,000 to £2,000,000.

Is travel delay covered?
Yes, but only if your flight is delayed for 12 hours or more due to mechanical breakdown, adverse weather or industrial action. The cover varies from £100 to £250 depending on the insurance company. Some cover your holiday costs if you abandon the holiday after a 12 hour delay, up to £5,000.

What happens if I miss the plane?
You are covered, but only if your arrival at the airport is too late to board the plane due to failure of public transport services, breakdown or accident in the vehicle in which you were travelling to the airport, and additional travel and accommodation expenses are incurred. The cover can be up to £800 depending on the insurance company.

What about legal advice and expenses?
Cover is provided for legal expenses resulting from a claim for compensation arising from the insured person's death or injury, generally up to £10,000.

Do insurance companies cover you for other things?
Some insurance companies provide hijack benefit, loss of passport expenses and catastrophe cover. These are not standard covers of the average insurance policy, but may be included.

BEING AWARE OF EXCLUSIONS AND EXCESSES

Examining insurance exclusions
Exclusions are things which insurance companies do not cover against and will not pay up for. Sometimes they attach certain rules to different aspects of the cover which must be adhered to, otherwise settlements will not be made.

Exclusions concerning medical claims
The majority of insurance companies will not pay up for:

- suicide
- injuries sustained or medical treatment needed whilst under the influence of alcohol or drugs
- people with HIV
- people travelling against medical advice.

Some will not insure against illnesses which existed prior to booking the holiday, or against pregnancy. Some insurance companies either do not insure persons over 65, or charge higher premiums, sometimes double the normal.

Dangerous sports exclusions
Many insurance companies do not insure against what they class as dangerous sports. These include:

- racing
- mountaineering
- some water sports
- riding motor bikes or mopeds.

Fragile articles
Most insurance companies will not insure fragile articles taken on holiday such as radio/cassette players, tapes and so on.

Abiding by the insurer's rules

In cases of loss of personal baggage, personal belongings and money, the insurance companies state that suitable care should have been taken to supervise the property. So if you leave a beach bag unattended on the beach or near the pool and return after a swim to find it gone, the insurance company will not pay up, because you have not taken adequate steps to protect it.

Obtaining evidence

All the insurance companies state that any losses or thefts must be reported to the local police. To obtain a police report following a theft can take up a whole day. Nevertheless, if you do not have a police report to support your claim, the insurance company will not pay up. Ask your holiday rep for help in reporting the theft.

If your suitcase goes missing, you must obtain a report from the airport and present it to the insurance company on your return.

Do make sure you obtain receipts for anything you have to pay for which is claimable on the insurance, whether it be replacement clothes if your suitcase is lost, or medicines from a chemist. Without them your claim is worthless.

Understanding insurance excesses

An excess is an amount of money set by the insurance companies on each claim which they will not pay, but the insured person has to pay.

Claims under most sections of holiday insurance policies are subject to an excess. It varies but is generally the first £35 of each claim. Excesses nearly always apply to the following sections of the insurance policy:

- personal baggage
- personal money
- medical and emergency expenses
- cancellation charges
- travel delay.

Avoiding excess charges

Some insurance policies give you the option of paying a supplement on the policy, so that if you do need to claim you will not need to pay the excess. This is called **excess waiver**.

This is a personal choice and whether it is a good idea or not will depend on how much the supplement is.

QUESTIONING FREE INSURANCE

Be very wary of free insurance. If you book through a reputable travel agent, the chances are you will not have any problems. However, there are some unscrupulous people about, and some insurance is not worth the paper it is written on.

To help safeguard against being given useless insurance make sure that you:

- ask to see a copy of the policy and check that you are covered at the very least for
  - medical expenses and emergency costs for a minimum of £2,000,000
  - cancellation and curtailment costs up to the final invoice cost of the holiday, personal baggage and money
  - personal accident with minimum cover of £15,000, personal liability and travel delay.

- ask who the insurance is through. If the name does not sound familiar, check them out to make sure they are reputable. You will find ABTA's address and telephone number listed under Useful Addresses.

- have received the insurance policy prior to your departure date, to take on holiday with you. You should do this anyway, but it is doubly important if the insurance is free.

- have it noted on your holiday invoice from the travel agent that the insurance is free. This is to avoid any later confusion as to who has paid for it in the event of claiming.

Assessing how 'free' the insurance is

Free insurance is certainly a sales gimmick. Whether it is actually free is debatable.

Certain conditions will be attached to free insurance deals, including the amount your holiday costs, and generally you must take the travel agent's insurance and not the tour operator's.

If you are tempted into booking a more expensive holiday because of the lure of free insurance, then you probably will not gain much more than if you booked a cheaper holiday and paid for the insurance. How much better off you are depends on how much you really want to spend and whether you have children travelling.

TAKING OUT THE AGENT'S OR OPERATOR'S INSURANCE

What is the difference between the two?

As far as the cover is concerned, there will not be much difference. The main difference lies in how much it will cost you to take out, and again this depends on several factors including:

- whether children are travelling with you
- whether people over 65 are travelling with you
- whether you want to participate in dangerous sports
- whether people with pre-existing medical conditions are travelling with you.

BEING INFLUENCED BY THE TRAVEL AGENT

There is no doubt that any good travel agent will try and sell you their insurance as opposed to the one offered by the tour operator, for example Thomson, Cosmos, First Choice and so on.

The only reason for this is that the travel agent receives a higher commission for selling an independent insurance, *ie* not attached to a tour operator, than if he sells a tour operator's insurance.

Insurance commission is one of the main methods a travel agent has of boosting his profits. It is possible for him to make four times as much profit by selling his own insurance as opposed to selling you the tour operator's insurance.

Travel agents can be very persuasive because of the financial incentives on offer, and every effort will be made not to sell you the tour operator's insurance. However, if the tour operator's insurance better suits your needs, insist on it.

Some of the big travel agency chains actually allow the staff to keep a percentage of whatever commission they make by selling independent insurance. So you can see why the pressure is so great.

In case of claims
If you return from holiday with an insurance claim, you may find that the travel agent will work harder on your behalf if you have taken out their insurance rather than the tour operator's. However, it is not uncommon for holiday representatives to work harder abroad for holidaymakers who have opted for the tour operator's insurance.

Getting a couple of quotes
The best thing to do is to get a quote for both the tour operator's and travel agent's insurance. Providing that the cover is comparable, then opt for whichever is the cheapest.

Exploring all options
If children are travelling with you, be sure to ask the travel agent about

family policies. Instead of charging individual prices for insurance, on family policies a set amount is charged for two adults and their children. This can sometimes be applied to grandparents and their grandchildren as well. Both tour operators and travel agents offer family policies, which can mean a substantial saving depending on how many children you have.

OTHER FACTORS CONCERNING INSURANCE

Taking insurance out when you book

If you put off taking out insurance until the last minute and you have to cancel the holiday due to one of the reasons listed on the insurance policy, you will not be able to recover the costs from the insurance company. So in effect you will finish up paying for a holiday which you cannot go on. This is because the nearer to the departure date you cancel, the more the tour operator will charge in cancellation fees.

Taking out the correct length of cover

As insurance cover generally applies to the number of days you are away, ensure that you have calculated the amount correctly. This is especially true on night flights. For example, if your holiday is for seven nights, but your return flight does not bring you back in the UK until the early hours of the next morning, then you will need nine days' cover and not eight.

This extra day could make a difference to the insurance premiums if it happens to fall into the next price group. Similarly, if something happens on the last day which is claimable, and you are a day short on the length of cover, the insurance will not pay up.

Checking the insurance policy properly

No matter what insurance you decide to take out, make sure that it suits your personal requirements.

CHECKLIST

- Do you understand what the insurance covers you for?
- Are you aware of the exclusions?
- Do you understand what excess you will pay if you claim?
- Are you aware of the conditions if the insurance is free?
- Is the free insurance with a reputable firm?
- Have you compared different insurance quotes?
- Have you checked that the insurance covers your requirements?

CASE STUDIES

Edward and Jean check their insurance carefully

As Edward and Jean travel abroad on holiday regularly, they are quite knowledgable about insurance, and if they are unsure about any aspect of it they do not hesitate to ask.

However, since they are both in their 60s, they always check the policies on offer, to ensure that they do not have to pay higher premiums. They also check that there are no exclusions because of pre-existing illnesses such as Jean's angina.

With these factors checked, they take out the best priced insurance at the time of booking their holiday.

Nancy pays more than she needs to

Nancy has never had to sort out holidays before. She asks the travel agent's advice about insurance, and is steered towards taking the travel agent's insurance. She does not compare the policy cover nor the insurance premiums with the tour operator insurance. This decisions results in her paying more for her insurance for not as good cover.

John and Susan decide against insurance

The travel agent tries to sell John and Susan his own insurance, on a family policy. This would be ideal for them, since the tour operator with whom they book their special offer does not offer family policies, only individual premiums, making it more expensive.

However, John rather foolishly decides against taking out insurance, claiming that the money he has saved will go towards more spending money for on holiday.

DISCUSSION POINTS

1. Prior to reading this chapter were you aware of the excesses charged by insurance companies? Do you think they are unnecessarily high?

2. Do you think the insurer's rules are reasonable? Which aspects of them would you alter and why?

3. What other things would you like to see insured on holiday insurance policies and why?

5
Understanding the Services of ABTA

ABTA stands for the Association of British Travel Agents. It was formed in 1950 with only 100 members; nowadays it represents 90 per cent of the travel agents and tour operators in Britain.

How does it work?
ABTA is a self-regulatory body run by its members. Travel agents and tour operator members choose a network of councils and committees to make policies, and ensure that they are adhered to. This enables ABTA to keep in touch with all its members, maintain high standards and improve conditions within the travel industry.

ABTA negotiates with British and overseas governments for reductions in airport delays and try to avoid air traffic control strikes.

REALISING THE IMPORTANCE OF ABTA

When booking a holiday it is essential that you choose a travel agency which is bonded by ABTA. This means that you will be protected financially should the travel agency go out of business before you travel. Or if you have already travelled abroad you will be brought back to the UK, without any further expense to yourself. If the travel agency is not ABTA bonded, and it folds, you will lose what you have paid for your holiday, or if you are abroad it could be very costly returning home at your own expense.

Knowing what to look for
Most travel agencies display the ABTA symbol (see Figure 9) on the premises. It generally appears:

- outside on the agency signs
- on the shop front door
- inside on a poster or as a certificate
- on the back of brochures on the shelves
- on office stationery such as letter heads, compliment slips, invoices
- as an official stamp showing the agency name, address and ABTA number.

If you are unsure whether the travel agent is a member of ABTA do ask, and they will be only too pleased to furnish you with the ABTA number if they have one.

Each travel agency has its own ABTA number which must be quoted when booking a holiday through the tour operators to prove their membership. Without this they are not allowed to sell their holidays. The majority of tour operators are also ABTA members and have individual numbers on their brochures.

Umbrella ABTA numbers
If a travel agency does not have an ABTA number or is waiting to receive one, sometimes they will use the ABTA number of another travel agency under an agreement amongst themselves. This is not legal and will not provide you with any protection.

If the travel agency does not display an ABTA number and cannot produce anything providing they have one, do not use them.

Fig. 9. The ABTA symbol.

Codes of conduct for travel agents

Once a travel agency becomes a member of ABTA, they have to adhere to strict rules laid down by the Association, which are agreed by the Office of Fair Trading.

The main aim is to provide high standards within the travel industry, which in turn is in the best interests of you the consumer. Some of the main features of the code of conduct are that it:

- regulates travel agents' actions towards their customers

- checks that the necessary paperwork is carried out and complied with

- checks that complaints are dealt with in the proper way

- ensures that agencies provide correct information to their customers on important subjects such as insurance, passports, visas, vaccinations and so on

- ensures that the agency has the correct number of qualified staff

- checks all members' financial accounts at least once a year, and imposes fines if they are not presented on time.

Codes of conduct for tour operators
Tour operators also have to operate by a code of conduct. Again this is to maintain high standards within the industry, which ultimately helps you the consumer.

Some of the important points are that:

- brochure descriptions must be accurate especially concerning travel arrangements, accommodation types, resort information and meal arrangements

- booking conditions found in all brochures are closely monitored, especially relating to the cancellation or alteration of holidays by the tour operator, after the customer has booked

- any complaints received by the tour operator must be dealt with promptly and efficiently.

Failure to comply with the ABTA regulations by both tour operators and travel agents results in a scale of fines depending on the degree of non-compliance. Therefore it is in their interests to abide by the rules, which in turn results in a better standard of service for you.

Educating staff
As all travel agencies must have some qualified staff as well as youngsters who are coming into the trade from school, ABTA takes this responsibility very seriously.

They run a selection of courses for members covering the different experience levels from trainee to management. This ensures that the highest standards of service are passed on to the consumer.

MAKING THE MOST OF THEIR SERVICES

In addition to raising the standards within the travel industry, ABTA also publishes lists of all travel agents and tour operators who are ABTA members. Their address and telephone number is listed in the Useful Addresses section.

Providing your financial protection
If a travel agent or tour operator who is a member of ABTA fails financially ABTA will:

● help customers who are already on holiday to continue with their holiday arrangements, as near as possible to their original plans, and ensure that customers are returned to the UK.

● reimburse payments made by those customers who have not yet embarked upon their holidays

To fund this financial protection, all ABTA members have to provide bonds to protect the customer in case of financial failure. There are also further funds which cover all members and so provide a safety net to support the bonding system.

ABTA travel agents mainly use tour operators who are ABTA bonded. Using a non ABTA member might result in no financial protection should the tour operator fail financially, even though the travel agent is a member of ABTA. Again check with them or with ABTA that your chosen tour operator is an ABTA member.

Travel agent's contributions
Each travel agency must provide the following financial requirements before an ABTA membership is granted:

● minimum bond level of £50,000

● working capital surplus of at least £15,000

● payment to the Travel Agents' Bond Replacement Scheme of £400 for each head office and £40.00 for each extra branch, and 2.5 per cent Insurance Premium Tax.

- registration fee of £330 plus VAT which is non returnable and payable when applying for membership

- entrance fee of £1,375 plus VAT which is payable upon admission to membership

- annual subscriptions of £500 plus VAT per company plus £120 plus VAT for extra branch offices

- paid-up share capital or capital account balance of at least £50,000. Total net assets after deducting intangible assets should not be less than £50,000.

ABTA's arbitration service

If you are unable to resolve a holiday complaint satisfactorily in the resort then your travel agent will usually deal with the tour operator on your behalf.

The tour operator is required by ABTA to reply fully to your letter of complaint within 28 days of receipt. If you do not receive a reply within that time advise ABTA. If you are not happy with the reply after two letters you can take matters further in one of two ways:

- claims under £1000 can be dealt with by the Small Claims Court

- alternatively ABTA offer an independent arbitration scheme administered by the Chartered Institute of Arbitrators.

If you are using the arbitration scheme, all applications must be made within nine months of your return from holiday. Application forms can be obtained from ABTA's Consumer Affairs Department (see Useful Addresses). A registration fee must be paid.

The service is designed to be simple, quick, informal and inexpensive. The final decision is made on documents only, so it is important to provide as much evidence as possible with your written statement of complaint.

CHECKLIST

- Is your chosen travel agent an ABTA member?
- Is it his own ABTA number?
- Is your choice of tour operator covered by ABTA?
- Are you aware of ABTA's services?

CASE STUDIES

Edward and Jean learn from experience

Edward and Jean are aware of the importance of booking only with travel agencies who are ABTA members.

This fact was demonstrated to them when they had booked in February one year to go to Italy in September of the same year, and in August the travel agent folded. However, because the travel agent was a member of ABTA their money was reimbursed – enabling them to book another holiday, with a minimum of inconvenience.

Nancy takes advice

Nancy is a little inexperienced when it comes to sorting out her holiday: prior to her divorce her husband made all the holiday arrangements.

She decides to watch some of the holiday programmes on the television to clue herself up on the subject, and also discusses it with friends, who advise her to make sure that she books with an ABTA travel agent.

With this information in mind, Nancy goes to sort out her holiday, ensuring that her travel agent is a member of ABTA.

John and Susan are lucky

As John and Susan have never been abroad before they know nothing at all about booking a holiday or anything associated with it. The most important thing in John's mind is to get a holiday as cheaply as possible. Where he books it will be determined by who offers him the best deal, irrespective of whether they are ABTA members. Susan will go along with what John decides.

By good fortune more than anything else, the travel agent who offers them the best deal does happen to be a member of ABTA. John and Susan, however, are none the wiser about ABTA's benefits, as they know nothing about it, and are not interested enough to ask the travel agent any questions.

DISCUSSION POINTS

1. Before reading this chapter, which services provided by ABTA were you aware of?

2. Which of our three sets of case study characters would you identify yourself most with?

3. Do you think that ABTA are strict enough with the codes of conduct for both travel agents and tour operators? What changes would you make if any?

6
Taking Children Abroad

As anyone who has been on holiday with children will tell you, it is entirely different from travelling with adults.

If you are to enjoy your holiday, you must make sure the children are catered for. You have a better chance of avoiding disaster with children if you prepare carefully before the holiday.

FINDING THE RIGHT DESTINATION

Many of the factors involved in choice of destination were covered in Chapter 2 in a general way. The main things to consider when taking children are:

- heat
- length of flight
- length of transfers to resort
- standard of medical facilities abroad
- suitability of beaches and other resort facilities.

Gathering information

The more information you can find out about the holiday, the happier you will feel when travelling with children.

Study plenty of different brochures to gain maximum information before reaching a decision. Different tour operators do provide different angles on different matters, and some feature more children's type holidays than others. Your local library should have books aimed at people travelling abroad with children, which can provide valuable advice and tips. Do not be afraid to ask your travel agent about any points you may be unsure of.

Children are welcome abroad
No matter where you choose to spend your holiday in the Mediterranean, children are made to feel very welcome. They are positively encouraged to visit restaurants and cafés even late at night, so you do not need to feel uneasy about taking them with you.

You may find that the locals appear to be a little over friendly with your children. This is just their way: many of them, especially the Italians and to a certain extent the Greeks and Spaniards, come from children orientated families and communities. No harm is meant by their behaviour.

DECIDING WHEN TO GO

If your children are under school age, avoid school holidays at all costs. Travelling during this time usually means:

- more chance of delays due to strikes
- high temperatures
- highest prices
- crowded resorts and beaches.

Under the 1944 Education Act, children can be allowed off school for up to two weeks a year. Many parents are not happy about taking their children out of school, but a lot of money can be saved and better deals struck by travelling during term time.

Considering children's ages

A child's age needs to be considered if taking them out of school, especially if it is at a crucial period such as a change of school or exam time.

Determining when you travel by the child's age can save you large amounts of money. This will be the case if:

- Your child is about to turn two years of age. By returning from your holiday before their second birthday, they will be classed as an infant and you will only pay approximately £19.00 (depending on the tour operator), instead of the child price.

- Your child is about to exceed the age limit for being classed as a child. The age limits vary depending on the tour operator and type of accommodation. By returning from holiday before that significant birthday, you will be charged a child price instead of an adult one, which will make a big difference to your cost.

CHOOSING THE RIGHT TYPE OF ACCOMMODATION

Choice of accommodation is covered in Chapter 3, but here it is considered from an angle of child suitability.

Matching accommodation with your child's age

Your choice of accommodation will be determined largely by the ages of your children. If you are travelling with babies and toddlers, self catering apartments can offer many benefits including:

- more freedom
- more room for their extra equipment and for play
- better facilities for heating and preparing bottles and food
- less embarrassment if they throw tantrums, so more peace of mind for you
- more flexibility at mealtimes
- a fridge for storing drinks.

For children possibly aged three and upwards, hotel accommodation may suit you more. The benefits could include:

- provision of buffet style meals, geared towards children's tastes, so they can choose what they want, and eat however much they want

- family rooms which offer more space when children are sharing with you (note that the number of rooms taking four or five people are limited and so early booking is essential)

- baby sitting services – sometimes there is a charge

- playgrounds and paddling pools and/or shallow part of the pool for children

- early mealtimes – check with individual hotel descriptions for details.

LOOKING AT ENTERTAINMENT AND ACTIVITIES

In hotels and some self catering accommodation both hotel chains and tour operators offer entertainment and activities for children. Some even offer facilities for babies and toddlers.

All about children clubs

Your children are in safe hands as the representatives in charge of the children have relevant experience and many of them are NNEB qualified.

Activities and entertainments are provided at the clubs for children up to 17. The clubs are split into age groups. There are many activities on offer such as Treasure hunts, sports, games, face painting and fancy dress.

The children can attend the clubs as often as they like. However, during peak times numbers may need to be restricted and sometimes there might be a rota. There is generally a maximum ratio of one representative to 15 children at the clubs.

Most clubs provide children with free T-shirts, badges, hats and so on. Check the individual brochures for which properties the clubs are held at. Figures 10 and 11 show tour operators and hotel chains which offered children's clubs in 1996. Details include the name of the club, age groups covered and where you can find them.

Suitability of children's clubs for your child

Whilst some children thrive on the clubs others are simply not interested. If your children are not interested in them, and you are not bothered about having a break from them, then there is no point picking accommodation with these facilities, since ultimately you pay more generally at accommodation where plenty of activities are provided.

These clubs can be ideal if you have just one child with you on holiday. They are an ideal way for them to make new friends and avoid boredom. It does, however, depend on the personality of your child.

THINGS TO CHECK BEFORE BOOKING

There are probably many things you want to check before actually booking your holiday. Here are some of the most common queries when travelling with children:

- Low floor rooms. Special requests can be made for low floor rooms if you are bothered about children climbing on balconies. Every effort is usually made to accommodate families on low floors, but it cannot be guaranteed.

- Adjacent rooms – if you have older children in rooms of their own, so you can keep an eye on them. Again every effort is usually made but cannot be guaranteed.

- Accessibility for prams: if there are lots of steps are there alternative entrances served by a lift?

- Will children sharing a room with you be in proper beds or are they expected to 'top and tail' (see Chapter 1)? Will this arrangement suit your child?

- Do you have to pay for cots and highchairs and is bed linen provided for the cot?

	Tour Operator				
	First Choice			Sunset	
Zante	X				
Halkidiki	X				
Tunisia	X				
Turkey	X				
Crete					
Kos	X				
Rhodes	X				
Corfu	X				
Cyprus					
Algarve	X				
Malta	X				
Costa de la Luz					
Fuerteventura	X				
Lanzarote	X				
Gran Canaria				X	
Tenerife	X			X	
Costa Blanca	X			X	
Costa Brava	X			X	
Costa Dorada	X				
Costa del Sol	X				
Costa de Almeria					
Ibiza	X			X	
Minorca	X			X	
Majorca	X				
Name of Club	Nippers	Surfseekers	Beach Hounds	Sammy's Troopers	Sammy's Rangers
Age range (in years)	3-6	7-11	12-15	3-6	7-11

Fig. 10. Tour operators offering children's entertainment in 1996.

	Tour Operator		
	Cosmos	Thomson	Aspro & Airtours
Zante		X	
Halkidiki		X	
Tunisia	X	X	X
Turkey	X		
Crete	X	X	
Kos	X	X	
Rhodes	X	X	X
Corfu	X		
Cyprus	X	X	X
Algarve	X	X	X
Malta	X	X	
Costa de la Luz	X		
Fuerteventura	X	X	X
Lanzarote	X	X	X
Gran Canaria	X	X	X
Tenerife	X	X	X
Costa Blanca	X	X	X
Costa Brava	X	X	X
Costa Dorada	X	X	X
Costa Del Sol	X	X	X
Costa de Almeria	X	X	
Ibiza	X	X	X
Minorca	X	X	X
Majorca	X	X	X

Name of Club	Sooty	Teen	Big T	Shrimps	Dolphins	Sharks
Age range (in years)	3-9	10-14	4-12	3-5	6-10	11-15

Fig. 10. Continued.

Hotel chain	Destinations	Clubs on offer	Activities on offer	Which hotels
Sol Hotels	Many Spanish mainland & Spanish island resorts. See tour operator brochures for details.	Club 4 age 1-4 yrs	Baby facilities Baby sitting, games	Sol Club Hotels Sol Family Hotels
		Club 8 age 5-8 yrs	Games, handicrafts, treasure hunts, discos	Sol Club Hotels Sol Family Hotels
		Club 13 age 9-13 yrs	Sports, disco, cabaret, competitions, video games	Sol Club Hotels Sol Family Hotels
		Club 17 age 14-17 yrs	Sports, competitions evening entertainment	Sol Club Hotels Sol Family Hotels
Med Playa Grupotel Globales Hotels Fiesta Hotels.	Many Spanish mainland & Spanish island resorts. See tour operator brochures for details.	See individual hotel descriptions for facilities and entertainments provided.		

Fig. 11. Hotel chains offering children's entertainment in 1996.

- What the bathroom contains: most have a bath with a shower over the top, but some have a bath or shower. Will the children be happy with the arrangements?

- Proximity of the beach: is it easily accessible with a pram? Is it sandy or shingle?

- Is the sea safe for swimming? Are there strong currents and tides?

SURVIVING THE JOURNEY

Taking extra equipment

No baggage allowance is given to infants as they only pay a nominal fee. However, a collapsible pushchair, food and nappies for the flight can be carried free of charge. Children do get the full baggage allowance, which is 15-20 kg depending on the type of plane.

As infants are the ones who need the extra equipment, space and weight is going to be at a premium, so pack carefully and only take what you definitely have to.

Again what you need to take will be determined by the age of your children. Don't take things which can be bought as cheaply abroad such as sun tan lotions. Certain baby items can be quite expensive abroad, such as nappies in Greece and jars of baby food in the majority of resorts abroad.

Make sure the items you need during your journey are in your hand luggage.

Minimising stress

The journey will probably be the most stressful time for you as parents, and the most boring time for your children. However, with careful preparation the stress and boredom can be greatly reduced.

Avoiding night flights
Avoid night flights if possible when travelling with babies and young children. Many people say children will be exhausted by the time they get on the plane and will sleep all night. This may be the case but it is just as likely that the different routine and excitement could mean them being hard work.

If your flight departs the UK at 2300hrs or midnight, the chances are it will not return until 0400 or 0500hrs (in the morning). As you have to be out of your accommodation by midday the previous day, to say the children will be exhausted and grumpy is an understatement. Admittedly the night flights will save you money, but you could be in for a very stressful and tiring time.

Dressing for the journey
Make sure that children are dressed in comfortable clothes for travelling. Dress them so that layers of clothing can be removed when you arrive abroad. Remember to pack an extra jumper or coat for the return journey, when they will notice the drop in temperature upon landing back in the UK. It can also be cold on the plane.

Being prepared for delays
Travelling midweek can cut down the risk of delays, but some delays are inevitable regardless of when you travel. You can make them more bearable by:

● taking some sandwiches to while away some time eating them – airports can be expensive places for eating at

● taking some sweets to occupy the children while they are waiting

● taking toys and books in their hand luggage.

If you are travelling with a baby, ensure that you have extra nappies and baby food in your hand luggage, in case of delays.

Some airports now provide play areas for children, which are ideal if there are delays.

If you are allowed to keep hold of your pram do so, so that if you are delayed the baby can sleep in it. Also it can be quite a walk to the departure gate, with a baby and hand luggage.

Checking-in early
By checking-in early you will be able to get the seats you want for your journey. The bulkhead seats on a plane are often given to families as they provide extra room. Many children like to have a window seat, or you may find it more practical to be seated near the toilets, to prevent having to walk the length of the plane.

Keeping children entertained
Many airlines provide children with colouring books, magazines and so on. Many have inflight entertainment on the headphones with a children's channel. Some airlines arrange for children to visit the flight deck if time permits during the flight.

Eating on the plane
Eating on the plane passes some time. Some airlines provide older children with meals catering to their own tastes, but this must be requested when

booking the holiday. If children's meals are not on offer, the food may not be to their liking. It may be a good idea to pack some crisps or favourite food in your hand luggage, so that they do not feel left out.

KEEPING YOUR CHILDREN SAFE AND HEALTHY

In the relaxed environment of your holiday destination, it is easy for children in unfamiliar surroundings to be exposed to unexpected dangers.

Some dangers to be aware of

- As hotel and apartments have no restrictions on people coming and going, be sure to emphasise the point about not talking to or going off with strangers.

- Many beaches abroad have jellyfish on them. Warn children about touching them. The holiday representative will tell you if there are jellyfish near your resort.

- Be sure children know which are the shallow and deep ends of the swimming pool.

- Many hotels have large plate glass windows/doors, often with no markings on them. Make sure your child is aware of this to avoid running into them.

- Check balconies to ensure children cannot squeeze through gaps in the railings.

- Ensure children are accompanied when using lifts, as many do not meet the same standards as British ones.

- Cots should be checked thoroughly for loose screws, flaking paint and holes in the wire mesh. Make sure it is deep enough to prevent the baby climbing out. Check that the mattress is thick enough not to slip through the bars.

- Ensure children are supervised in the sea especially if they are playing on inflatable toys. Ask about strong sea currents.

Avoiding illness

The different diet, water and heat abroad can lead to health problems.
Taking the following precautions can reduce the chances of it happening:

- Avoid drinking local water, even if told that it is alright. Children probably won't like the taste anyway. If you are staying in apartments boil it first, buy bottled water, or use sterilising tablets.

- Avoid ice for the same reason as freezing the water does not kill the bacteria.

- Ice cream should be avoided if possible: if it is allowed to melt and is then frozen, harmful bacteria can be present.

- Warn children against touching or stroking cats and dogs because of the threat of rabies.

- Keep children covered with sun cream as much as possible. Some are waterproof which is ideal when swimming. Sun hats are a must as well.

- Encourage children to drink as much as they like to avoid dehydration in the hot weather.

- Avoid eating shellfish due to the presence of harmful bacteria.

CHECKLIST

- Will the children's needs be met in your choice of destination?
- Is there a better time to go abroad other than when you have chosen?
- Do you know where the accommodation is located?
- Will the accommodation facilities suit you as a family?
- Are entertainments and activities important to your children?
- Have you made a note of special requests for when you book?
- Have you made a note of any questions to ask the travel agent?

CASE STUDIES

John and Susan are travelling blind

They have certainly not considered the children at all. By opting for a special offer the chances are it will be a night flight. They do not know exactly where they will be staying in Majorca, so the transfer could be quite long. They will not know which accommodation they will be staying in until they arrive, therefore they do not know if it is suitable for children. They are going in the school holidays so it will be very hot. Self catering may be a good idea with taking the baby, but the elder children may be bored, depending on how many facilities the apartments have.

DISCUSSION POINTS

1. Despite their limited funds, how could John and Susan have avoided a potentially disastrous holiday with their children?

2. Which factors do you consider to be important for your particular family holiday, when deciding where to go and what type of accommodation to stay in?

3. What questions do you want to ask your travel agent about your holiday with children?

7
Making the Reservation

UNDERSTANDING THE BOOKING CONDITIONS

It is very important that you understand exactly what you are agreeing to when you book your holiday. Most people sign the booking form blindly, understanding little. Many travel agents do not explain the importance of the booking process.

Before booking your holiday, turn to the back of the brochure, where you will find the booking conditions. Study them carefully and ask your travel agent if you are unsure about anything.

Different tour operators use different terminology for 'booking conditions', so other titles could be:

- consumer protection plan
- fair trading charter
- fair trading agreement
- code of conduct.

It all amounts to the same thing: when you sign the booking form, you make a commitment to the tour operator, and when they accept your booking, they make one to you. It is a two way deal in which the interests of both parties are protected.

What is the tour operator's commitment?
Over the years the booking conditions have become a lot easier to understand, using simple clear vocabulary.

Generally the tour operator promises:

- to book and confirm your choice of holiday and forward a holiday invoice

- not to increase the price of your holiday once it is confirmed; however, if there is a reduction in the total cost, this will be passed on to you

72

- that if they cancel your holiday you can have a full refund or choose another one, and compensation will be paid to you (if the reason for cancellation is beyond their control, no compensation will be paid)

- that if they change your holiday after it is confirmed you can either accept the new arrangements or choose another holiday, and still receive compensation

- to sort out any complaints you may have

- to provide the services that you have booked regarding hotel and so on; if they fail to do this and it spoils your holiday, compensation will be paid

- to pay for any injury, illness or death caused by using the services organised through the tour operator

- to help to sort matters out in the case of injury, illness or death not connected with the tour operator's arrangements.

What is your commitment?

The rules do vary between the tour operators but generally you must:

- pay a deposit when you book the holiday

- agree to pay the amount shown on the holiday invoice sent by the tour operator, at least eight weeks before your departure date

- advise your travel agent if you wish to make any changes to your booking such as departure date, hotel and so on. If the details can be changed an amendment fee will be charged (see Chapter 8) for each person travelling and each detail you change. There must be more than six weeks left prior to the holiday, otherwise you will have to pay cancellation charges

- advise your travel agent in writing if you have to cancel your holiday. Cancellation charges will be imposed (see Chapter 8). The amount you lose is determined by how close it is to the departure date

- advise the holiday representative if you have any complaints. If it is not possible for them to sort out the problem abroad, they will make out a report which you sign; it must then be taken up with the tour operator on your return

- not cause any disruptive behaviour on the plane, as the captain has the right to refuse your entry (if this is the case your holiday is cancelled and all monies will be lost)

- not to let people stay in your holiday accommodation other than those listed on the booking form.

CHECKING AVAILABILITY

Providing alternatives

When you are choosing your holiday do not just pick one holiday and expect it to be available, especially if you can only travel on a certain date.

If you want a specific hotel or apartment, check several brochures as quite often they are featured by numerous tour operators. Remember the cheaper holidays and the ones offering free and greatly reduced child places will be booked up very quickly, especially for popular dates. So alternatives are essential if you are going to get a holiday you want.

Saving time at the travel agents

If you can travel on alternative dates take a list with you so they can be checked, listing them in order or priority. Similarly make a list of alternative hotels/apartments in case your first choice is full. The more alternatives and choices of holiday you have, the better chance you will have of getting fixed up, and the more time you will save in the travel agents.

You will also save time if you can advise the travel agent which flight you require: if travelling to Majorca, for example, there may be a choice of four flights, all departing on the same day.

Going in person

The travel agent will check to see if your different holiday choices are available with the tour operator directly via the computer. If none of your choices is available the computer will provide a list of the nearest alternatives with the same tour operator.

Travel agents will check availability if you phone rather than go to their shop, but at busy times people in the shop will generally get priority over telephone customers.

Holding options

Travel agents will not book your holiday unless you are in the shop with your deposit. However, some tour operators will hold your chosen holiday for 24 hours, so that if you have enquired by phone, you then have time to get to the travel agents to book. This is called 'holding the holiday on option'.

This option also allows you to discuss with other party members any alternatives offered by the travel agent.

If you want the holiday it must be booked and a deposit paid within 24 hours, otherwise the option will expire automatically, and the holiday will go back on sale.

CONFIRMING THE HOLIDAY

Once you have decided definitely on your holiday, the travel agent will ask you if you wish to confirm it. Once you say yes, the travel agent confirms it with the tour operator via computer. Make sure that all the names you give for the booking are spelled correctly. Completing this stage means that a contract has been made between yourself and the tour operator, and you are committed to paying for that holiday. You cannot change your mind now without incurring further costs.

Making special requests

Be sure to tell your travel agent about any special requests when you book your holiday. Whilst the tour operator will not guarantee any special requests, every effort is usually made to provide them.

Some of the popular requests can be made directly via computer at the time of confirming the holiday. Others, such as specific seats on the plane due to physical disabilities, usually need to be made in writing to the tour operator. Similarly, if you are taking drugs or medicines on holiday with you, it is advisable to inform the airline of the details to avoid being questioned at the airport. Your travel agent will be able to do both these things on your behalf, if you bring it to their attention when booking.

COMPLETING THE PAPERWORK

Checking the booking form

Once the holiday has been confirmed by the travel agent, they will complete a booking form on your behalf for your holiday. This contains all the details which the travel agent has fed into the computer. Be sure to check the following carefully:

- date of departure
- departure airport
- holiday duration (length of stay)
- name of hotel or apartment
- resort
- titles, initials and surnames of all passengers
- ages and dates of birth of children

Departure airport	Departure date	Resort	Hotel/apartment

Duration	Flight Code	Accommodation code	Booking reference

Board SC BB HB FB 1st Room/apartment PB WC BL SV (delete)	Address to which correspondence will be sent or travel agent stamp ABTA No Your ref

Title	Initial	Surname	Age	Date of birth	Ins
					Yes Yes Yes Yes Yes

2nd Room/apartment
PB WC BL SV (delete)

Title	Initial	Surname	Age	Date of birth	Ins
					Yes Yes Yes Yes

Special requests

Insurance
Travel insurance is strongly recommended. You will be automatically covered by our insurance unless you delete YES above. If you are arranging your own insurance, please provide details here:

Insurance company: Policy number:

Total deposit paid   £

I have read and understood the booking conditions and accept them on behalf of all persons listed.

Signed   Date

Fig. 12. Sample booking form.

- total deposit
- insurance details (see below).

Figure 12 shows a sample booking form.

If there are any mistakes on the form, make sure you tell the travel agent immediately. If you do not then the incorrect information will come through on your holiday confirmation, and the tour operator is entitled to charge fees to correct mistakes.

Insurance

Make sure that you check which insurance arrangements have been made on the booking form. Your travel agent should discuss this with you. The word YES usually appears after each person's name on the booking form (see Figure 12). If you wish to take the tour operator's insurance, then leave YES showing. If you want to take the insurance on offer from the travel agent or an alternative insurance the YES must be deleted (some tour operators require the name and policy number of the alternative insurance you will be taking).

If the YES on the booking form is not deleted, then the tour operator insurance will be automatically added to your holiday invoice and you will have to pay for it even if you don't need it. It is your responsibility to check the booking form before signing it.

Responsibility for signing the booking form

The person who needs to sign the booking form is the person whose name is first on the form; this is known as the lead name. The booking will be confirmed under this name.

The person who signs the form is responsible for making the payments for each of the other members listed on the form.

Paying the deposit

Once the booking is confirmed a deposit must be paid to the travel agent. The amount you pay is set by the tour operator and will vary between £70 and £80 per person.

A deposit must be paid for each person listed on the booking form, the only exception being infants. If you have a free child place, a deposit must be paid when booking and this will be deducted from the balance of the holiday.

Deposits can usually be paid by cash, cheque or credit card. They are non refundable. They are only recoverable if the reason for cancelling the holiday is claimable via the insurance (see Chapter 4).

Paying for the holiday on time

Once the holiday is confirmed the tour operator will send you a holiday invoice via your travel agent. This displays all the details which should be carefully checked. It also tells you when the balance of the holiday is due to be paid.

The tour operator normally wants the money at least eight weeks prior to your departure date. However, the travel agent may ask you to pay him another two weeks earlier. He will claim that he needs time to clear your money and pass it onto the tour operator by the eight week deadline. In effect many travel agents use this as an excuse to improve their cashflow and make extra interest on your money.

Paying late

If you do not pay the balance of your holiday by the agreed date, then the tour operator has the right to cancel your holiday and impose cancellation charges, as you have broken your agreement.

The nearer to the departure date it gets, the greater the cancellation charges will be (see Chapter 8).

MAKING A LATE BOOKING

Questions and answers

What is a late booking?

A late booking is a holiday which is booked within eight weeks of departure.

Can I take out an option on a late booking?

No, options are not given on late bookings so a decision has to be made instantly.

When do I pay for my late booking?

The booking must be paid for in full there and then.

How late can I leave it before I book?

Bookings can be made right up until the day of departure, providing you have enough time to get to the airport to catch the flight.

What happens if there is not enough time to receive my travel tickets?

If your travel tickets have not arrived at the travel agents by the time you travel or if you book late, arrangements can be made to collect the tickets from the airport. Tour operators have desks there for this purpose.

CHECKLIST

- Do you understand the booking conditions?
- Have you made a list of alternative holiday choices?
- Do you understand about 'holding options'?
- Do you understand the importance of confirming the holiday?
- Have you checked the insurance details box?
- Have you remembered to make any special requests?
- Have you checked all the details before signing the booking form?
- Do you know when you have to pay the balance?
- Do you realise the penalties of paying the balance late?

CASE STUDIES

Edward and Jean plan carefully

As Edward and Jean are regular travellers, they understand the booking conditions, but they still check them before booking just in case any changes have been made.

Since they travel out of season and can be fairly flexible with their dates, they do not tend to make long lists of alternatives. They go to the travel agents together, so that if their original choice is full they can decide there and then about alternatives. The higher class hotels are not booked up as quickly as cheaper ones. They already know which other tour operators feature the hotel they want, since they study all the brochures to get the best flights and prices.

Edward usually signs the booking form and checks all the details before doing so. He isn't afraid to ask the travel agent any questions. He is always keen to know what date he must pay the balance of his holiday, before he receives the holiday invoice, and notes it in his diary. The travel agent can give him this information as it is displayed in the computer when the holiday is confirmed.

Nancy holds an option

As Nancy works full time out of town, she cannot call into the travel agents during the week. She doesn't like studying brochures and so doesn't know about the booking conditions. She lets the travel agent choose a suitable holiday for her, but when she looks in her handbag she realises that she has forgotten her cheque book and credit cards.

As the travel agent won't confirm the booking without a deposit and Nancy is unable to return to the shop during the week, he suggests holding the holiday on option for her. This secures the holiday until Monday when Nancy can phone the details of her credit card through to the travel agent, and he will confirm it. After completing the booking form Nancy signs it. Apart from the main details she doesn't really know what she is signing for.

Nancy explains that she is a vegetarian and so the travel agent requests vegetarian food both on the plane and in the hotel on the booking form and via the computer.

John and Susan blunder through the booking

John and Susan find a special offer and decide to book it. The travel agent completes the booking form for them, while Susan is stopping the children from fighting. John does not even check the form and just blindly signs it, as he is in a rush to get to the football match and is already late. As a result he does not notice that an initial is wrong in one of the children's names.

He tells the travel agent about his special requests but as he has booked a special offer, he is not allowed to make them. He will be lucky if he can remember what date he is travelling, let alone understand any booking conditions.

DISCUSSION POINTS

1. What do you think the consequences will be of John not checking the booking form before signing it in the case studies?

2. Do you think that the tour operator's booking conditions are fair? If not which conditions need to be altered and in what way would you change them?

3. Do you think the 'holding options' system is beneficial to you the customer? How do you think it could be improved?

8
Cancelling or Amending Your Holiday

UNDERSTANDING CANCELLATION CHARGES

Everyone hopes when they book a holiday that they will not have to cancel or alter it; however, circumstances may arise which mean you have to. So it is as well to know what is involved and where you stand if you find yourself in this situation.

If you find you have to cancel your holiday, the tour operator will make a cancellation charge. This covers the cost of processing your cancelled holiday and also compensates the tour operator in the event of him not being able to resell it.

Calculating the cancellation charges

The cancellation charge you pay is determined by how near to the departure date it is: the closer it is the higher the charges.

The charges do vary a little between the tour operators but Figure 13 shows some typical cancellation charges. They are usually shown as a percentage of the total holiday cost, but exclude insurance premiums.

The person who signed the booking form is responsible for paying the cancellation costs. It is important to remember that these charges also apply if you fail to pay for your holiday in time, and as a result the tour operator cancels your holiday.

Cancellation received in writing	*Amount payable (shown as % of total holiday price excluding insurance premiums)*
More than 42 days before departure date	Deposit only
29 - 42 days	50%
15 - 28 days	70%
1 - 14 days	90%
Departure date	100%

Fig. 13. Typical cancellation charges.

CANCELLING YOUR HOLIDAY

Cancelling your holiday must be done in writing by the person who signed the booking form.

To cancel the holiday the travel agent will either:

- write a letter of cancellation himself, which will contain all your holiday details, and ask the person to sign it who signed the booking form, or

- complete a cancellation form provided by the tour operator containing all your holiday details, and ask the person to sign it who signed the booking form.

Sometimes holidays can be cancelled directly through the computer, but the travel agent will still need written evidence that the holiday is to be cancelled.

If you have booked directly with the tour operator then you will have to write yourself to them, advising of the cancellation.

Once the tour operator has it in writing that the holiday is to be cancelled, he will send a cancellation invoice advising you of the charges incurred.

Part cancellation

If only one or more members of the booking have to cancel but the rest of the party is still travelling, it may mean, especially in the case of an apartment, that the accommodation is then under occupied. If this is the case the cost may be increased for the remaining party members. Those who have to cancel will of course lose their deposits and be subject to cancellation charges, depending on the proximity to the departure date.

CLAIMING CANCELLATION CHARGES THROUGH INSURANCE

If the reason for cancelling your holiday is covered by insurance, then you can claim the costs back through them. However, this only applies if you have taken insurance out prior to cancelling the holiday.

You can usually claim for the following reasons:

- illness or injury making travelling not possible
- death of a close relative near to the travel date
- jury service
- redundancy.

As insurance policies do vary, check your cover carefully to see exactly what you are covered for (see Chapter 4).

Making a claim

To recover costs you will have to complete an insurance claims form. When you cancel your holiday your travel agent should apply for one from the insurance company, or may have them in stock.

You will need to return the completed form to the insurance company with:

● the booking invoice showing the insurance premiums
● the insurance policy if you took out the travel agent's insurance
● the cancellation invoice received from the tour operator.

Providing evidence
If the cancellation is for medical reasons, you will have to ask your doctor to complete the medical section of the claims form, and he is entitled to charge you for this. If you have cancelled due to the death of a close relative, a death certificate must be provided. If redundancy has caused cancellation, evidence from your employer will need to be sent.

Failure to provide the relevant evidence or to complete the claims form correctly will usually result in a delay in settling the claim.

CANCELLATION BY THE TOUR OPERATOR

Tour operators will always try to provide you with the holiday you have booked. However, if there are not enough people booked on a holiday the tour operator has the right to cancel your holiday.

They will not cancel your holiday less than eight weeks before you are due to travel. The only exceptions to this are in the event of war, riots, political unrest, fires and health risks: in other words circumstances beyond the tour operator's control.

Considering the options available

If the tour operator has to cancel the holiday you have booked you can either:

● have a full refund, or
● choose an alternative holiday.

Receiving compensation

Whichever option you take, most tour operators will pay you compensation as well, unless the circumstances are beyond their control.

The amount of compensation you receive is determined by how close to the departure date the cancellation is. The closer it is the greater the amount of compensation. Compensation rates vary among tour operators, so be sure to check the booking conditions prior to booking.

AMENDING YOUR HOLIDAY

Understanding amendment fees

If you find after you have booked the holiday that you need to change any of the details – for example departure date or accommodation – you can, subject to availability, but the tour operator will charge an amendment fee for doing so to cover administration costs.

Many tour operators will not allow you to change any details within six weeks of your departure date and will class it as a cancellation and impose the relevant charges. Others will permit the changes but will charge higher amendment fees for doing so.

Calculating the amendment fees

Amendment fees do vary among tour operators. Some charge a fee of £15.00 per person named on the booking form and for each detail which is changed. Others charge £15.00 per booking for each detail which is changed. Some charge £10.00 per person but up to a maximum of £40.00 per booking form.

Make sure you check with the individual tour operator's brochures for details.

Making amendments

If you wish to change any details of your holiday, you must do so in writing.

The travel agent usually completes the relevant forms which contain the original details and the revised details, and then asks the person who signed the booking form to sign the amendment form.

The amendment fees usually need to be paid at the time of changing the details.

If you have booked directly with the tour operator, you will need to write to them directly, advising them of the changes.

Changes made by the tour operator

Due to the brochures being prepared a long time in advance, it is sometimes necessary for the tour operators to make minor changes to your holiday. They are quite entitled to do this and will advise you of changes through your travel agent.

Changing flight timings
The flight timings which appear in the brochures are only intended as a guide, and may change nearer to your departure date. They should keep you informed of any flight timing changes. The flight timings which appear on your tickets will be the actual flight timings.

Making major changes
Occasionally tour operators do have to make major changes to your holiday, such as:

- changing the resort area
- changing the UK departure airport
- changing your departure or return flight by more than 12 hours
- changing a day flight to a night flight
- changing the accommodation to one of a lower standard
- changing the length of your holiday.

The tour operator will inform you as soon as possible of the change via the travel agent, or to you if you have booked directly with them.

Considering the options
If a major change is made to your holiday, you have the following choices:

- accept the change made as advised
- choose another available holiday from the brochure
- cancel the holiday and receive a full refund of all monies paid.

Paying compensation
In addition most tour operators will pay you compensation for major changes. The amount they pay varies from £5.00 to £100.00 per person. The nearer the change is announced to the departure date, the higher the rate of compensation. However, compensation is not payable if:

- the tour operator has to make the changes due to circumstances beyond their control, such as war, riots, political unrest, fire, health risk, technical problems

- the tour operator informs you of the major change more than 56 days prior to your departure date.

Check with the booking conditions for your chosen tour operator to see how much they will compensate you if a major change should occur.

CHECKLIST

- Do you understand why cancellation charges are imposed?
- Do you know what percentage of cancellation charges you will pay?
- Do you know how to cancel your holiday?
- Are your cancellation charges claimable through insurance?
- Do you know how to make the claim?
- If cancellation is by the tour operator do you know how much compensation you will receive?
- Do you know how much it will cost to amend the holiday?
- Do you know how to amend your holiday?
- Do you know what the tour operator classes as major changes?
- Do you know what your choices are following a major change?
- Do you know how much compensation you will receive?

CASE STUDIES

Edward's and Jean's plans are upset

Edward and Jean are looking forward to their holiday in Turkey. However, four weeks before their departure date the travel agent advises them that the tour operator has had to change their hotel due to overbooking.

They go to the travel agents to see if an alternative tour operator can offer them the same hotel. Eventually they manage to get this offer, but departing a few days later than originally planned. They then advise the travel agent that they no longer wish to continue with the original holiday and will accept the alternative one. The travel agent carries out their instructions, and advises them that they will also receive compensation, due to the major change imposed by the tour operator.

Nancy changes her dates

Due to unusually bad weather, the tennis tournament which Nancy has been playing in is delayed, and so she will now have matches to play when she should be away on holiday.

She decides to delay her departure date for two weeks. Fortunately she knows about this more than six weeks before her departure date, and so has to pay just the standard amendment fee. She completes the relevant forms at the travel agents, and the date is changed accordingly.

John and Susan pay for not checking

The holiday invoice arrives for their holiday and Susan opens it while John is out. She spots that the initial is incorrect on their eldest child's name. She tells John later, and he immediately phones the travel agent, accusing the clerk of putting the wrong initial down on the form. The manager then advises John that he had better call into the shop, since he is to blame for not checking that the booking details were correct.

John has calmed down by the time he reaches the travel agency. He is none too pleased when the manager tells him that he will have to pay an amendment fee to correct the initial. He still fails to see why the wrong initial was his fault, even after several explanations. However, he realises that he is not going to receive his holiday tickets until he pays the fee, and so reluctantly pays it.

DISCUSSION POINTS

1. Before reading this chapter, which factors were you aware of regarding cancellation/changes made by the tour operator to your holiday booking?

2. In what way would you alter the conditions relating to cancellations and amendments generally, and why?

3. What do you want to ask your travel agent about cancellations and amendments to holidays?

9
Searching for Special Offers

GOING ABOUT IT

A special offer is a holiday which has been reduced in price from what it was in the brochure. You have to be prepared to spend a long time sitting in a travel agents while they find you a special offer. It is worth bearing the following points in mind:

- You are better going to a travel agency rather than phoning, because by the time you arrive there after being told there is something available, it could have gone.

- There isn't much to be gained from trekking around the travel agents, since they all receive the same special offers from the tour operators. For special offers it is the tour operators who do the discounting, not the travel agents.

- You need to be in possession of a full valid passport as there may not be time to obtain one.

- You need to pay the full cost of the holiday before the travel agent will book it for you. If you are offered a special offer and then have to go and get the money, it could have already gone.

- Depending how close it is to the departure date, if there is not enough time for a cheque to clear, the travel agent will want payment either by cash or credit card which can be cleared straight away.

- All persons who need to be present in making the decision should be at the travel agents, otherwise again whilst you are trying to contact the other party members, the holiday could go.

When to start looking
How early you should start looking depends on how popular the dates are

when you plan to go, and what the availability is like for your chosen dates.

Looking three weeks prior to your departure date will give you an idea of what is available and the sort of price you can expect to pay.

Many people think that the longer you wait the cheaper the holiday will become. This is not always the case because if there are not many holidays for your chosen dates, the prices will not be reduced.

ASSESSING THE DIFFERENT SPECIAL OFFERS

All travel agents receive special offers through the post every week, and the special offers are updated on the computer daily.

There are many different types of special offer:

- Some tour operators simply take a fixed amount off the brochure price, for example £20, £30 and so on per person. This type of offer means you know exactly where you will be staying as you can see it in the brochure. These special offers give you peace of mind, but not vast savings.

- Some tour operators list hotels or apartments in, for example, Majorca, and guarantee that you will be staying in one of those properties. Again you have some security in knowing that you will stay in one of these properties. You will save a little more generally from this type of offer.

- Some tour operators state the standard of accommodation you will be staying in, for example two star hotel, and guarantee you will stay in perhaps one of four resorts on that island. This sort of deal will generally save more money still.

- The special offer which saves you the most money is where you know you are flying into, for example, Ibiza or Malta, but you do not know where you will be staying until you arrive at the airport abroad. A hotel holiday will usually carry a minimum rating; self catering, however, will usually be cheaper, but no standard of accommodation is usually stated.

- Some tour operators sell just flight seats at the last minute, which can be greatly reduced. However, you then have to find your own accommodation, and also get a transfer to and from the airport. This can be very costly depending on your resort's proximity to the airport.

Choosing what is right for you

Make sure you understand fully the type of special offer you are booking.

The travel agent should go through the details with you, and complete a booking form as with a brochure price holiday.

No changes
Once a special offer has been booked, it cannot be altered due to it being a matter of weeks or even days to the departure date.

Taking children
If you are travelling with children, you will probably get a better deal out of the brochure with child reductions. Holidays on special offer do not allow much extra in child reductions.

Am I really getting a bargain?
This is the question that most people ask themselves when they are looking at a special offer.

There is an element of luck with special offers. Some are genuine bargains, while with others the savings are debatable.

Whether you feel you have got a bargain is largely determined by:

● Where you end up on the holiday. Some people will be put in a hotel which suits their every need; others will be put in one which does not suit them at all.

● Which resort you stay in. Again what suits one set of holidaymakers will not suit another.

● How flexible you are. The more open minded you are, the less disappointed you will be.

● Your attitude. People who go on special offers expecting five star hotels in the top resorts will certainly not feel they have got a bargain. Those who take the attitude that you get what you pay for will not be disappointed.

● The time of year when you travel. Travelling out of school holidays generally produces better deals and offers.

● The amount of surplus holidays the tour operator has at any given time. This is governed by the laws of supply and demand. If there are not many places left on the plane, then the prices will not be reduced. However, if the plane is half empty, prices will be lowered in an attempt to recover losses.

Settling for second best

What most people fail to realise about special offers is that they are the holidays which are left because other people do not want them.

It may be simply that the tour operator has over-estimated his capacity levels for that particular time of year. Equally so the hotel or resort where you finish up could be one of those which is not very popular for whatever reason, and so is filled up by special offers.

How much you save will determine whether you would have been better having the holiday that you want out of the brochure, rather than the holiday others do not want at a reduced price.

ASSESSING THE PROS AND CONS

Advantages

The advantages of special offers can be:

● bargains can be found if you are in the right place at the right time

● for people on a limited budget, it may mean the difference between going abroad or not

● they are more suited to adults travelling on their own in small numbers – for example, it is easier to pick up two seats on a plane and a twin hotel room than four seats on a plane and a family hotel room.

Disadvantages

The disadvantages of taking special offers can be:

● not knowing which resort or accommodation you are staying in
● many special offers tend to be on night flights
● children's needs will not necessarily be met
● the elderly or disabled may find themselves in unsuitable locations
● you might not get the dates you want if you have set holidays
● you spend a lot of time in travel agents waiting to get fixed up.

UNDERSTANDING AGENTS' DISCOUNTS

Agents' discounts are reductions or other incentives offered by the travel agents to try and tempt you into booking your holiday with them as opposed to another travel agency.

Considering what is on offer

Agent discounting generally reaches its peak in January, when people have put Christmas behind them and their thoughts turn towards summer holidays.

Competition amongst the travel agents is fierce in an attempt to increase their share of the holiday market.

Some of the incentives to gain your holiday booking may include:

- percentage discounts: the more you spend, the greater your discount
- reduced deposits: perhaps only £5.00 instead of £70.00 – £80.00 per person
- free insurance (see Chapter 4)
- delayed payment scheme: book now and pay later
- discount food vouchers
- free beach items
- holiday savings clubs.

Remembering the conditions

You may think initially what wonderful discounts and offers the travel agents are making. However, there are usually conditions attached, which might include the following:

- You must take out the insurance on offer from the travel agent (see Chapter 4).

- You must sign an indemnity form if paying a low deposit, which holds you to paying the remainder by the specified date.

- You must spend a minimum amount before discounts apply.

- You will be charged interest if you do not pay by the specified date on the delayed payment scheme.

- Money which has been saved in holiday savings clubs will not normally be refunded, and must go to the holiday cost or towards spending money in the form of travellers cheques or foreign currency.

Before agreeing to any of the discounts or offers from travel agents, make sure you know which conditions apply.

SEEING THROUGH THE SALES PLOYS

Not many people give things away for nothing, and the same is as true in the travel industry as in any other.

Giving discounts

If the discount on offer carries the condition of taking the travel agent's insurance, be very wary. The compulsory insurance may not be the best one for your needs, and it could cost a lot more than the alternatives. This could well mean that the amount you are saving is not the attractive sum you originally thought it was.

Offering low deposits
Again with low deposits, often the travel agent's insurance is compulsory, and the remainder of the deposit has to be paid within three months anyway. So you are not gaining a lot here since the balance on the holiday will still need to be paid eight weeks prior to your departure date. In effect you have been forced into taking out insurance which isn't necessarily the best or cheapest, for the sake of delaying the deposit for a few extra weeks.

Giving free insurance
You may be tempted into opting for a more expensive holiday by the promise of free insurance if you spend over the limit set by the travel agent.

Again this can be false economy, because by paying for a less expensive insurance with another travel agent and not being forced to spend a set amount of money per person, the overall cost can work out cheaper.

Providing savings clubs
By paying money into a savings clubs, you are paying for your holiday before the date when it is due, and the travel agent is making interest on your money. If you saved the money in your own building society account, *you* would receive the interest.

Receiving good discounts or service
If you start exploring the world of agents' discounts, it will become clear that it is the large chains of travel agents who offer the largest discounts, for example, Lunn Poly and Going Places.

This is because the large chains are only interested in getting what they call market share, the more passengers they can book the better.

Many of them will push certain tour operators more than others, because of the higher commission incentives they are offered.

As a result of their strategies, many of the multiple travel agents are not very helpful when it comes to giving the customer information or advice which is not available from the brochure.

Trying the independent travel agents
This is where the independent travel agent scores over large multiples. While the small independent cannot compete with the financial incentives, he can offer extras in the way of guidance, advice, service and information. They do not have very high sales targets to hit every week, and so can

afford to spend time with you, finding out what you want and not what they wish to sell you.

CHECKLIST

- Do you understand what a special offer is?
- Do you know how to get a special offer?
- Are you aware of the different types of special offer?
- Is a special offer suitable for your needs?
- Do you realise what the advantages and disadvantages of special offers are?
- Do you know what agents' discounts are?
- Are you aware of the different choices on offer?
- Are you aware of the conditions which apply to them?
- Are you actually gaining anything from the discounts?
- Are you aware of the different types of travel agent?
- Are discounts or service more important to you?

CASE STUDIES

Edward and Jean want the personal touch

Edward and Jean are not interested in discounts and special offers. They want to choose their holiday from the brochure, and be able to ask the travel agent any questions they might have. They find that the independent travel agency has more time to spend with them, and provides the personal touch which they find is lacking in the large multiple travel agencies.

Nancy gets a discount

Nancy decides to book her holiday in January, so that she has plenty of time to save up for it. As she books at the time when all the travel agents are competing for business, she is offered a percentage discount. To receive the discounts, however, she must take out the insurance on offer from the travel agent, at the time of booking. As Nancy isn't used to arranging holidays, she decides that as she will need insurance anyway, she might as well take advantage of the discount on offer.

John's and Susan's special offer

As John and Susan wait until the last minute for a special offer, they have missed out on the agents' discounts which were available earlier in the year.

They trek around the travel agents in town looking for a special offer. John is too impatient to sit in the travel agency while they check through the availability. He would sooner leave his name and telephone number for them to contact him. However, Susan is worried that they are not going to get a holiday.

Eventually, one of the agencies comes up with a special offer in Majorca which they can just about afford, but John has not brought the full amount for the holiday with him. He promises to return that afternoon with the payment if the travel consultant will book it, so that they do not lose the holiday. She explains that she cannot do that as it is a special offer, nor can she hold the holiday. John is furious and storms out of the shop to go and raise the money. When he returns later fortunately the special offer is still available, which he books.

DISCUSSION POINTS

1.   Where did John and Susan go wrong regarding finding a special offer? How would you have gone about it?

2.   Do you find the agents' discounts confusing? If so what measures should be taken to simplify them?

3.   Which factors are more important to you when choosing a travel agent, better discounts or service?

10
Obtaining Passports, Visas and Vaccinations

APPLYING FOR A PASSPORT

As British Visitors Passports have now ceased to be valid for travel abroad, anyone going abroad must apply for a full **ten year passport**.

The following question and answer section explains many of the issues when applying for a passport.

Questions and answers

Where can I get a passport application form?
You can get one from main post offices and travel agents.

Which form do I use?

● If you are over 16 you will need form A.
● For a passport for a child under 16 you will need form B.
● To make changes or add children to a passport you will need form C.
● If you wish to apply to extend a passport you will need form D.
● If you wish to apply for a replacement passport you will need form R.

How do I apply?
When you get a passport application form an addressed envelope is provided. Post it when completed. If time does not permit this, you can apply in person but do not be surprised if you have to queue. You will find a list of addresses and telephone numbers for the passport offices under Useful Addresses.

When should I apply?
Ideally as soon as you know you will be going abroad. If you apply between September and December a passport can usually be arranged within two weeks; between January and August it can take four weeks or more. Your nearest passport office will advise you how long applications are taking at that time.

Can I get a passport quickly?
If you can prove by means of your travel ticket that you need a passport quickly, it can usually be arranged. It can be done either in person at the passport office or by post.

How much does a passport cost?
The cost for a ten year passport is currently £18.00.

How do I pay?
Do not send cash if applying by post. Cheques or postal orders are acceptable. If you are applying in person at the passport office you can pay by cash, cheque, postal order, debit or credit card.

Completing the forms

Before starting to complete the form, make sure you read the notes which are enclosed. This will avoid you making mistakes as they can be a little complicated.

Before sending off the completed form, make sure that you have:

- completed all the relevant sections
- signed the declaration
- enclosed the necessary documents (originals not photocopies)
- enclosed two photographs
- enclosed the fees.

Failure to either complete the form correctly or enclose the necessary documentation will only result in a delay in processing your application.

Ensuring children have passports

Any child under the age of 16 needs to be mentioned on a passport in order to go abroad. They can be included on their parents' passports, but make sure that you apply to add them well in advance. It is strongly recommended to have children listed on both parents' passports, then in the event of injury or illness abroad, children can travel with either parent.

Having a passport of their own
Children can have a passport of their own. If they are over 16 or are going to travel without you then they must have one.

FURTHER MATTERS ABOUT PASSPORTS

It is your responsibility to ensure that you have a valid passport for your holiday. There are other rules and regulations concerning passports which you should be aware of.

Losing your passport

If you lose your passport or have it stolen whilst abroad, you must contact the British embassy or consulate immediately. They will check your identity and arrange for you to return home by temporary documents. Once home, you will have to reapply for a new passport.

Ensuring names match

It is very important that the name and initial on the travel ticket match those on the passport. If they don't you may be unable to travel when they are checked at the airport, and your insurance may be void.

If your tickets do appear with the wrong name, return them to your travel agent who will advise the tour operator; they will be reissued, but charges could be incurred.

Checking the validity of your passport

Certain countries require that your passport must be valid for at least six months after your return date. This is the case if travelling to Egypt, Cyprus or Morocco. If you are travelling to Gambia, your passport should be valid for a minimum of three months after your return.

You should check with your travel agent as the rules are subject to alteration.

Having foreign stamps in your passport

Some foreign stamps in your passport can cause problems when visiting certain other countries. The main examples of this are:

● visiting Egypt and your passport has an Israeli stamp
● visiting Cyprus or Greece and your passport has a Turkish Cypriot stamp
● visiting Arab countries and your passport has an Israeli stamp.

If any of the above apply to you, it is advisable to contact the passport office, as you may need to obtain a supplementary passport.

Holding a non-British passport

The information in this chapter is for British citizens only. All other countries should check with the embassy of the country they wish to visit and the Home Office Immigration Department to see if any special documents are required for visiting those countries and for returning to the UK.

ORGANISING VISAS AND VACCINATIONS

Do I need a visa?

Some countries state that you do need a visa to gain entry. Figure 14 shows which countries require them, where you apply and how much they cost.

Country	Visa obtained from	Cost
Turkey	On arrival in Turkey	£10.00 (payable in English notes)
Egypt	Egyptian Embassy 2 Lowndes Street London SW1X 9ET. Tel: (0171) 235 9719.	£15.00
Israel	Israeli Embassy Consular Section 2 Palace Green London W8 4QB. Tel: (0171) 957 9500.	£8.00

Fig. 14. Visa information and costs.

It is your responsibility to ensure that you have any necessary visas, so be sure to ask your travel agent for up to date information, since visa requirements do alter. Allow plenty of time for the processing of visas, as long delays can occur at peak times and if you are not in possession of a British passport.

Applying for a visa
The visa application form should be obtained from the relevant embassy, by phone or post. It should be completed and returned to the embassy with any required documents and fee.

Some visas are issued on a separate piece of paper which you place in your passport, others are stamped in it. The embassy will advise you if they need your passport.

Some travel agents will apply for the visa on your behalf, others expect you to apply on your own. Some tour operators will make arrangements for issuing visas, many will not.

Which countries require which vaccinations?
Different countries have different requirements concerning vaccinations. You are advised to check with your GP who has up to date lists of vaccinations and the countries for which they are necessary.

Allowing enough time
It is important to plan your vaccinations at least two months prior to departure. This is because:

- some require a course of injections which have to be given with so many days or weeks between each injection

- some produce side effects which you will need to recover from before travelling abroad

- you may have to travel to a specialist centre for certain vaccinations, and so will need time to organise them

- some vaccinations cannot be given at the same time as others.

How much will they cost?
Some of the vaccinations such as typhoid and hepatitis are free on the NHS if your GP does them. Others can incur a charge. You should check out the costs for your requirements as some of them can be £25.00 each. The more unusual ones can be costly and have to be done at a specialist centre. Anti-malaria tablets can be purchased over the counter, but check which type you need as there are different types.

Getting them done
The main places for obtaining vaccinations are your GP, travel clinics and specialist clinics. Make sure you keep the certificate of vaccination and take it with you on holiday.

CHECKLIST

- Have you checked to see if your passport is still in date?
- Have you used the correct passport form?
- Have you completed the form correctly?
- Have you enclosed the required documentation and fee?
- Have you checked that your children are mentioned on passports?
- Have you allowed enough time for your passport application?
- Have you checked if you need a visa?
- Do you know how and where to apply for your visa?
- Have you allowed enough time to obtain your visa?
- Are vaccinations necessary for your holiday destination?
- Have you allowed enough time for your vaccinations?
- Are you aware how much they will cost?
- Do you know where you can have the vaccinations done?

CASE STUDIES

Edward and Jean require visas

Edward and Jean have valid ten year passports and so do not need to worry about applying for new ones.

They have found out that they will require a visa, but that it can be purchased on arrival in Turkey. They are also aware that it must be paid for with English notes and so plan to set aside £20.00 in English money for this purpose.

They have also checked with their GP, who has advised them to have hepatitis A, polio and typhoid vaccinations, and are making arrangements for them.

Nancy needs a new passport

Nancy's passport has expired and she decides to apply for a new one when she books her holiday. As she is not used to doing things like this, she asks the travel agents for advice and they give her the relevant form, and answer her questions. The travel agent checks the completed form for her and she sends it off to her nearest passport office.

As she is going to Crete she does not need any visa or vaccinations.

John and Susan waste a lot of time

As John and Susan have never been abroad before, they do not possess passports. However, John insists that they do not waste money on passports until they have booked a holiday. Because they left it to the last minute to get a special offer, they cannot apply for a passport by post – there are only four days left before their departure. Consequently they have to go to the passport office, spend all day there queuing, only to be told that they will have to come back the next day and collect it. This is due to John failing to complete the forms correctly. As a result John and Susan have a big argument.

They are travelling to Majorca so no visas or vaccinations are necessary.

DISCUSSION POINTS

1. How could John and Susan have avoided their predicament at the passport office?

2. Do you think passport application forms should be made easier to understand? If so, how?

3. Do you think passport information should be available in more places? If so where would you like to see it displayed?

11
Hiring a Car Abroad

Car hire is becoming increasingly popular when travelling abroad as a means of exploring independently, rather than taking organised tours. It provides freedom to visit places off the beaten track when you want, and for how long you want.

NEEDING A CAR OR NOT

In some properties and resorts hiring a car is a necessity, if only to gain access to the nearest civilisation for your basic groceries.

This is especially true of private villas and even some apartments. Many of the brochures indicate that car hire is essential if staying in these properties. Some even include it in the prices for so many days, but many leave it to you to arrange.

Your type of holiday

Whether you hire a car will depend on your type of holiday. If you are happy to stay around the pool and beach, with the occasional trip out, then hiring a car would prove expensive and a waste of time. If you enjoy exploring and seeing as much of the country as possible, then hiring a car can add a further dimension to your holiday.

BOOKING HERE OR ABROAD

Many of the car hire firms in the UK claim that their prices are the cheapest and generally it is cheaper to book before you go.

Which of the different options is the best for you depends mainly on how long you want the car for. You may require it for all the time you are abroad, or just for one or two days. Where you want to collect the car will also make a difference to booking car hire.

Booking before you go

The advantages of pre-booking your car hire in the UK are:

- Sometimes there are special offers from the car hire firms/tour operators which may not apply abroad. These can include free car hire on certain dates and, for example, 'four days for the price of three' at certain times of year.

- Your car is guaranteed, which it isn't if you book when you arrive abroad.

If you book car hire before you go on holiday, you have two options:

- book through an independent car hire company such as Avis and Hertz, or
- book through the tour operator with whom you have booked your holiday.

Your travel agent can make the reservation for you.

Booking independently
If you book through an independent car hire company, you pay for the car hire before you go abroad. This saves having to take large sums in foreign currency with you to pay for the car abroad.
    If you book independently normally you must:

- book the car for a minimum of three consecutive days
- collect the car from and return it to the airport
- pay extra if the car has to be collected outside office hours
- pay extra if you want to have the car delivered to and collected from your holiday accommodation (not always available).

Booking through the tour operator
If you book car hire through the tour operator with whom you have booked your holiday, your normally pay a deposit at the time of reserving your car and the balance in the resort. Most tour operators will guarantee the car hire price in local currency, which also means you will know how much foreign money to take to pay the balance.
    This option may prove a little more expensive than dealing direct with the car hire company, since the tour operators will add a commission to the price for arranging the car hire on your behalf.
    If you book through the tour operator normally you must:

- book the car for a minimum of three consecutive days
- have the car delivered to and collected from your accommodation
- give at least seven days notice prior to your departure.

Booking car hire abroad

The advantages of booking car hire abroad can be:

- you can usually hire the car for as little as one day
- you can decide whether you want a car once you have seen where you are staying
- you can arrange to share car hire with people you meet at the resort.

You usually have two options as to where to book car hire:

- through the holiday representative who visits your holiday accommodation
- through a local car hire firm in the resort.

Booking through the holiday representative
Your holiday representative can normally make arrangements if you want to hire a car. This will generally be more expensive, since they will charge a commission for arranging it.

This option is usually the safest, since you know exactly who you are dealing with, and they generally use reputable car hire firms. All the negotiating is done for you.

Booking through a local car hire firm
If you have plenty of confidence or have travelled a lot, you might enjoy the challenge of booking car hire with a firm in the resort. It is advisable to stay with the reputable, well known companies to avoid trouble.

It will probably work out cheaper, since the car hire firms are all in competition, putting you in a good bargaining position. If negotiating on your own, make sure you are fully aware of what the prices includes.

UNDERSTANDING WHAT YOU GET FOR YOUR MONEY

When hiring a car it is very important that you understand what is included in the price, so that you are not in for any surprises when you collect the car.

What is included

Generally the following things are included in the cost:

- unlimited mileage
- third party insurance
- collision damage waiver (CDW – see below)
- bail bond in Spain

- local taxes
- collection to and from airport or holiday accommodation.

Make sure you check when booking, as different car hire firms may have slight variations.

What is not included
Generally the following things are not included in the car hire price:

- personal accident insurance (PAI – see below)
- petrol
- delivery/collection out of office hours
- optional extra including child seats and roofracks
- additional driver charges
- theft protection
- car contents insurance.

Understanding the car grades
When you book a car you will be asked what size of car you require. This will depend on how many people there are in your party, and the amount of luggage you will have if collecting from and returning to the airport.

Again there is some variation between the car hire companies and indeed the different countries, but generally there are three or four car groups, group A being the smallest and C or D being the largest.

Examples of the car makes and models for each group are shown in the price panels. The prices are normally displayed for three or seven days hire. Extra days can usually be quoted upon request.

Figure 15 shows a sample car hire price panel, using Ibiza as an example, displaying the car groups, makes and prices. The prices are in local currency and sterling: if you book car hire through the tour operator, you need to know how much to pay locally, and how much that is in English money.

If you book independently through the car hire company the prices will be quoted in sterling, since the full amount is paid here before travelling.

TAKING YOUR DRIVING LICENCE

To hire a car abroad you must take your driving licence, as you will not be allowed to hire one without it.

When you collect the car, everyone who is named as a driver on the car hire form must show their British driving licence. You must have held the licence for at least one year before you can hire a car.

Car group	Car type or similar	1 May–30 Jun 1 Oct–31 Oct		1 July–30 Sep	
		3 Days	7 Days	3 Days	7 Days
A	Ford Fiesta Opel Corsa Fiat Punto 3 dr	12850 (£69)	24900 (£134)	13350 (£72)	26300 (£141)
B	Peugeot 106 Fiat Punto 5 dr Citroen AX 1.4	14200 (£76)	28250 (£152)	15350 (£82)	30100 (£162)
C	Ford Escort Renault 19 Opel Astra 4 dr	16350 (£88)	33250 (£179)	17100 (£92)	35450 (£190)

Prices shown in Spanish pesetas and pounds sterling in brackets

Fig. 15. Sample car hire price panel for Ibiza.

Knowing the requirements

To hire a car abroad drivers must be at least 21; however, the following countries have minimum age requirements:

- Cyprus: 22 with an upper age limit of 75
- Portugal and Madeira: 23
- Italy and Turkey: 25
- Morocco: 25 with an upper age limit of 65
- Malta: 25 with an upper limit of 70
- Ibiza and Costa del Sol: 25 years with an upper limit of 79.

Types of driving licence

If you have the old style green driving licence, it may be advisable to change over to a pink one before going abroad. This can be done at the post office by completing a form.

If you hire a car in Spain or Italy and have the old green driving licence, they will also wish to see an International Driving Permit. These can be obtained from the AA (see Useful Addresses).

Young drivers

In some countries a surcharge may be imposed on young drivers if they are hiring one of the larger cars. Check with the individual car hire companies.

Endorsements

Similarly if you have any endorsements on your licence, you should advise the car hire company when booking as refunds will not be given later.

CONSIDERING OTHER MATTERS

Taking out PAI

PAI stands for Personal Accident Insurance. When you hire a car, you will be asked if you require it at an extra cost. This is not usually necessary as your holiday insurance normally covers you.

Understanding CDW

CDW stands for Collision Damage Waiver and is included in most car hire prices. If you are responsible for an accident in the hire car, you are protected against the cost of any damage to the car by CDW. The CDW basically makes third party insurance into fully comprehensive. It does not cover against theft of and vandalism to the car. Separate cover must be taken out for this.

Leaving a deposit

Most car hire companies require you to leave a deposit to cover petrol and local charges.

The best way to do this is to leave the deposit in cash or travellers cheques. Sometimes you do not have a choice, as some car hire companies insist that a credit card is used. Avoid paying the deposit by credit card if possible, as it means you have to sign the credit card voucher leaving the amount box blank. This leaves you in a vulnerable position if things go wrong with the car hire.

Providing petrol

Most car hire companies either:

● charge you for a full tank of petrol when you collect the car, and you bring it back as near to empty as possible (refunds are usually given for unused petrol) or

● provide you with a full tank of petrol when you collect the car, and you must pay to fill the tank up again when you return the vehicle.

Some of the less reputable firms have been known to tamper with the fuel gauges so that the fuel tank seems fuller than it is. This is another reason for booking through a reputable firm.

AVOIDING DISASTER

When hiring a car you want to avoid disaster if at all possible. Your chances will be greatly improved if you:

● hire from large reputable companies: the prices may be a little higher, but the cars will probably be newer and safer and you will probably find them easier to deal with in a dispute

● check that the car is roadworthy before driving it away: check for bald tyres, make sure lights and brakes work properly

● check the paintwork for any dints or scratches

● make sure the car can be locked properly

● ask for a test drive before leaving the car hire office if you are not happy with the vehicle

- seek advice about what to do if the vehicle breaks down and how to claim the expenses back.

CHECKLIST

- Are you aware of all the car hire booking options?
- Do you know what is and is not included in your car hire price?
- Do you understand the car hire grading system?
- Are you aware of the driving licence requirements?
- Do you know how to avoid disaster?

CASE STUDIES

Edward and Jean hire a car

Edward and Jean always hire a car – they like the freedom and the ability to explore.

They prefer to book and pay for the car hire through one of the reputable car hire firms, when they book the holiday. They find this more convenient since they do not have to take large sums of currency with them. They book a group A car as there are only two of them. They collect and drop the car off at the airport, to save having to do a tour of the hotels on the coach.

Edward always checks the car thoroughly before leaving the car hire office, and asks questions about anything he is unsure of.

Nancy does not need a car

Car hire does not appeal to Nancy as she is a nervous driver and does not relish the idea of driving abroad.

She is quite content to relax in the sun, play sports and swim. If she wants to see any local sights, she will go on one of the organised excursions.

John and Susan can't afford it

The idea of hiring a car certainly appeals to John but their limited funds will not allow it.

DISCUSSION POINTS

1. What questions would you want to ask about hiring a car abroad?

2. Do you find the different booking options confusing? If so what would you do to simplify them?

3. Is there anything not already included in the car hire price which you think should be?

12
Sorting out Foreign Currency

Many people ask, especially first time travellers, which am I better taking: travellers cheques or foreign currency?

The best advice is to take both. Take the bulk of your money in travellers cheques and a small amount to get you through the first few days in foreign currency.

Taking travellers cheques

The advantage of taking most of your money in travellers cheques are:

- it is safer – if they are lost or stolen you will be able to get them refunded
- you are not carrying large amounts of cash with you.

The disadvantages of taking most of your money in cash are:

- the insurance company will cover you for only a limited amount of cash
- there is no proof you ever had the cash
- keeping it safe whilst you are abroad
- if you are mugged you have no other finances to fall back on.

BUYING TRAVELLERS CHEQUES

Travellers cheques can be purchased over the counter at most bureaux de change and travel agencies. You can obtain them through your bank or building society, but they will probably need some notice.

When you buy your travellers cheques, you will be asked to sign:

- each one of the cheques in front of the person who sells them to you
- another slip which has a record of your travellers cheque numbers on it.

You will be given a copy of the slip. Take it on holiday with you, but keep it separate in case your travellers cheques get lost or stolen. You can then advise the issuing company of the stolen numbers. There are usually instructions on the reverse of the slip explaining how to obtain a refund.

Choosing which denominations to take

Travellers cheques come in a range of denominations: for example, pounds sterling cheques start at £10 and go up to £200.

It depends how much money you take with you, but you are better to have mainly £50 cheques and a fewer lower denominations, for example £20 and £10 cheques as well. This is because at the end of your holiday you might only want to change £10, and if you only have £50 travellers cheques you will be stuck with extra foreign currency which you neither need nor want.

The advantage of having the higher denominations is that you will be charged less commission. So for example if you were to take £200 in 4 x £50 travellers cheques, you would not be charged as much commission as if you took 20 x £10 travellers cheques. This may sound a little miserly, but costs can soon mount up with all the transactions you make whilst abroad.

Choosing which name to put them in

When couples and families go abroad, one person is usually in charge of the finances, and that includes sorting out the travellers cheques.

Whilst most people opt for this plan, it is not the ideal way to do it. It is far better for each adult in the party to have travellers cheques in their name. The reasons for this are:

● if one person's cheques are stolen, you have the other person's travellers cheques to fall back on until a refund is sorted out

● if one person is taken ill or has an accident on holiday, the other person still has access to some money.

Obtaining foreign travellers cheques

Many foreign exchange places now offer travellers cheques in both pounds sterling and the currency in which you will be dealing abroad.

Currency travellers cheques are usually available in:

● Cyprus pound
● French franc
● Spanish peseta
● Swiss franc.

You may have to order these foreign currency travellers cheques, so allow extra time.

It is advisable to ask whether you will obtain a better deal by purchasing foreign currency travellers cheques, as opposed to sterling ones. A lot will depend on the strength of the pound at the time and where you are going. With these type of cheques you can see how much foreign currency you will get for each cheque.

CASHING TRAVELLERS CHEQUES

When you cash a travellers cheque it is important to remember that:

● they can be cashed only by the person whose name they are in

● the person who signed for them when they were purchased must countersign them in front of the person who is cashing them, and the signatures must match

● you must sign the travellers cheque only when cashing it in case it is lost or stolen

● sometimes further identification can be asked for when cashing them such as your passport.

Paying commission

When you buy travellers cheques and foreign currency you will be charged a commission by the vendor. Some charge a set rate, others charge a percentage on the sale. Make sure you know how much you will be charged before buying them.

You will pay a lot more commission if you change your money in your hotel rather than in a foreign exchange centre or bank. However, many hotels offer a 24-hour cashing facility, so you are paying for that convenience. You also know it is there in an emergency.

It is a good idea to find out the opening hours of the banks, to avoid paying higher commissions in the hotels.

DEALING WITH LOST OR STOLEN TRAVELLERS CHEQUES

If you are unfortunate enough to have your travellers cheques lost or stolen, replacements can be arranged by the issuing company.

When they issue you with the travellers cheques, you should be informed about the procedure to follow in order to have them replaced. Make sure you take this information on holiday with you.

Keeping a record

The replacement process will be speeded up if you have kept a record of the cheque numbers which you have spent, and the ones which have been stolen. This is easily done as when you purchase your travellers cheques you are usually provided with a separate blank form. You should fill this in every time you cash a cheque, so that you have a record.

You are also given a slip of paper which contains your cheque numbers, which you keep separate from your cheques. You then have a record of the numbers in the event of them being lost or stolen.

UNDERSTANDING FOREIGN CURRENCY

What currency do I need?

Before you can purchase any foreign currency you will need to know what the currency is for your chosen destination. Figure 16 shows the main package deal countries, currencies and exchange rates.

Country	Currency	Exchange rate
Austria	schilling	15.30
Bulgaria	lev	Restricted currency
Cyprus	pound	0.7075
Egypt	pound	4.7
France	francs	7.52
Greece	drachma	370.00
Israel	shekel	4.58
Italy	lire	2360.00
Malta	lire	0.545
Morocco	dirham	Restricted currency
Portugal	escudo	229.00
Spain	peseta	185.00
Switzerland	franc	1.785
Turkey	lira	93818.00
Tunisia	dinar	Restricted currency

Fig. 16. Countries, currencies and exchange rates as at 9/2/96.

The exchange rate for the foreign currency you will be using will give you an idea of the amount of currency you will be given to the pound. You will need to check nearer to your departure date to find out the exact exchange rates, as they do change daily.

Restricted currencies

Some countries – for example, Tunisia, Morocco and Bulgaria have what are known as restricted currencies. This means that the currency cannot be taken into or out of that country.

Converting foreign currency

When spending foreign money it is easy to spend it without thinking how much a particular item has cost, as you would do with English money.

In order to know the cost of things abroad you need to take a calculator. The method of calculating how much something costs in English money is shown below:

$$\frac{\text{cost of item in foreign money}}{\text{exchange rate}} = \text{cost in English money}$$

For example, if an item cost 7450 Greek drachmas, the calculation, based on an exchange rate of 370 Greek drachmas to the pound, would be:

$$\frac{7450}{370} = £20.14$$

CHECKLIST

● Are you aware of the advantages and disadvantages of taking travellers cheques?
● Do you understand about the different denominations of travellers cheques?
● Are you aware of the availability of foreign travellers cheques?
● Are you aware that commission is charged on travellers cheques?
● Do you know how to convert foreign currency to English pounds?
● Are you aware that lost or stolen travellers cheques can be replaced?

CASE STUDIES

Edward and Jean are organised

Edward and Jean always take travellers cheques on holiday, and a small amount of foreign currency to help them through the first few days.

They split the travellers cheques between them and have some in each name. Edward always takes his credit card with him to use in emergencies.

Early on in the holiday they familiarise themselves with the places which provide the best rates of exchange, and use them throughout their stay. They never use the hotel for foreign exchange, due to the poor rates.

They both keep a record of their cashed travellers cheques, and take a calculator with them to give them an idea of their spending.

Nancy opts for currency

As Nancy is going on an all inclusive holiday, she decides not to take any travellers cheques, since most things are included in the price.

She decides to take some foreign currency abroad for any excursions and purchasing presents. She plans to take her credit card to cover any unexpected expenses, but does not intend using it unless really necessary.

John and Susan take a risk

As this is their first trip abroad, the travel agent tries to persuade them to take travellers cheques and a small amount of foreign currency.

John says he cannot be bothered messing about with travellers cheques, and decides to take his entire spending money in English cash, as he things he will get a better exchange rate for pound notes. He cannot see any point in taking foreign money, when he can change some as soon as he arrives abroad.

Neither John nor Susan have credit cards and so have nothing to fall back on.

DISCUSSION POINTS

1. What problems could John and Susan encounter as a result of how they have chosen to take their spending money abroad?

2. Do you think that travellers cheques and foreign currency should be available in more outlets? If so which ones?

3. Would you like to see commission rates clearly shown in establishments which sell foreign currency and travellers cheques? Do you think it should be compulsory?

13
Making the Most of Your Holiday

UNDERSTANDING THE REPRESENTATIVE'S ROLE

Greeting you at the airport

Once you arrive at your foreign airport, the first English speaking person you meet will be your holiday representative. They will show you which coach to board for your transfer to your holiday resort. They usually provide you with plenty of information during your journey.

Dealing with missing luggage

If your suitcase is missing, advise the holiday representative who will help you with the Property Irregularity Form and Customers Declaration Form, which have to be completed before you leave the airport. Often the suitcase will turn up within the next few days, but if it doesn't you will need these documents to make an insurance claim for both delayed and lost baggage.

Organising the welcome meeting

Soon after your arrival, the representative will organise a welcome meeting. You are usually given a free drink to get you in the holiday spirit. Depending on the personality of the representative the meeting can be quite entertaining; it will, in any case, serve the following purposes:

- provide you with resort information
- highlight places of interest
- organise car hire
- sell excursions
- offer advice and tips.

You will be urged to attend the welcome meeting by the representative *en route* from the airport; it will be useful for the first time traveller especially.

Similarly if it is your first visit to that particular country or resort, you will probably find the information of interest.

Providing resort information

A good representative should be able to provide information on the resort's history, local attractions, sights worth seeing, local transport, taxis, beaches, dangerous sea currents and so on.

Do not hesitate to ask your representative any questions, as they are usually approachable, and will usually find out the answer if they do not know.

Beware of their recommendations for restaurants or bars in the resort, since they will probably be receiving commission. It will not guarantee good food or service.

Organising car hire

Your representative can usually organise car hire (see Chapter 11).

Selling excursions

Your holiday representative will try their best to sell you the company's programme of excursions. Most of them are employed on a basic wage, and can boost their income by receiving a commission for selling excursions.

There is usually quite a varied list of excursions on offer. Typical day trips include historical sights, waterparks and excursions around the island. At night barbeques and beach parties are popular.

Getting value for money

The barbeques can be a bit of a lottery as to how much value they represent. Often food can be a little scarce whilst local wine, which can be an acquired taste, is plentiful.

Doing it yourself

Whilst some excursions do represent value for money, some are expensive, and can be done cheaper using local transport. If there are a few people wanting to visit a particular place it may even work out cheaper to split the cost of a taxi between you.

The advantages to organising your own trips can be:

- you get better value for money
- you can go on the trip at your own convenience
- you are free to spend as much time at the place as you want.

Controlling your spending

After listening to the sales talk from the representative, some holiday-makers, after a few glasses of sangria, get carried away and sign up for numerous trips. Most trips are payable in local currency meaning that a lot of people spend more than they intended to, especially first time travellers.

Offering advice and tips

A good representative will be able to provide some useful advice and tips to make your holiday safer and more enjoyable. Subjects often include drinking local water, avoiding sunburn, buying goods from gypsies and so on.

Sorting out problems

If you encounter any problems whilst abroad, the holiday representative will usually try to sort them out for you. They could include:

● being robbed or mugged
● being ill and needing medical advice or attention
● losing luggage
● having to return to the UK early
● running out of money whilst abroad
● getting into trouble with the police.

Let the representative know as soon as there is a problem, rather than letting it spoil your holiday. More often than not they can help, and that is what they are employed for.

If it is your first time abroad, you may feel isolated if things go wrong, and the holiday representative acts as a lifeline for people in this position.

Returning you to the airport

Your holiday representative will advise you of the pick up time for your return trip to the airport on the notice board in reception. He or she will usually accompany you to the airport, find out which desk your flight is checking-in at, and sometimes assist with the check-in.

GENERAL PLANNING TIPS

You may find these general tips useful in planning for your holiday:

1. Many airports are known as silent airports: no boarding calls are made. You must watch the computer screens in the departure lounge to find out when to board the plane.

2. Do not put camera film in your suitcase, as new screening equipment has been installed at many airports, both in the UK and abroad, which can damage it.

3. Make sure you pack all electrical items and medicines in your hand luggage.

4. Divide the party's clothes among your suitcases, so that if one case goes astray everyone will still have some clothes to wear.

5. Make a list of the contents of your suitcase so that you don't leave things behind and if it goes astray it will be easier to make an insurance claim.

6. Do not display your home address on your suitcase luggage labels when departing on holiday; this can be an open invitation for burglars.

7. Take a basic first aid kit such as paracetamol, plasters and insect bite cream with you.

8. Pack some plastic carrier bags for dirty washing and wet swimming costumes.

9. Take any free samples of soap and shampoo as they are usually in small amounts and so don't take up too much room.

GENERAL HOLIDAY TIPS

You may find the following general tips useful whilst actually on holiday:

1. Inspect your accommodation before you unpack, ensuring everything is in working order.

2. Avoid buying from hotel shops which are generally expensive as they are used to dealing with tourists who are not familiar with the currency.

3. If eating out, go where the locals eat, and you will get better food at a cheaper price.

4. If you are phoning home, use public telephones not the hotel phone as they are very expensive.

5. If you are self catering in Greece, you are not allowed to put toilet paper down the toilet, due to the atrocious plumbing. It must be put in a bin and emptied daily.

6. When you land at the airport, there is no point rushing to get off the plane, as you only have to wait for your luggage and for everyone else to get on the coach.

7. If using taxis always agree on a fare before commencing your journey.

8. If visiting churches, women are advised not to wear shorts and to cover their shoulders, otherwise admission may be refused.

9. Be careful when taking photographs abroad, especially in Africa. You are not allowed to photograph government buildings and many military objects. People should not be photographed without their permission.

CHECKLIST

● Are you aware that you are met at the airport?
● Are you aware that a welcome meeting is held where you are staying?
● Do you know what the welcome meeting is about?
● Are you aware that they provide advice and holiday tips?
● Are you aware that they can help with problems or complaints?

CASE STUDIES

Edward and Jean seek information

Because Edward and Jean are collecting their hire car from the airport, they see the representative only briefly to let her know they had arrived, and do not go on the coach to the hotel.

As this is their first visit to Turkey, they are keen to find out as much as they can about the country and so attend the welcome meeting. They are not interested in going on any of the excursions, but keep the places being visited in mind to see at their leisure. Edward asks the holiday representative questions after the meeting and receives some useful tips and advice.

Nancy books some trips

As Nancy is on holiday alone, she goes to the welcome meeting to see if there are any other people in a similar position. She books a couple of excursions, as she doesn't want to venture out on her own. The excursions are ideal for her, as she can still visit places but with the safety of being with other people. She opts for a full day island excursion and an evening barbeque trip.

John and Susan overspend

John wants to go to the welcome meeting, not for the advice and information, but for the complimentary sangria.

By the end of the meeting John has consumed large amounts of sangria and thinks every trip seems like a good idea. Susan tries to rein him in because of their limited funds, but as usual John's decision is final. He books four trips for the whole family.

Three days into the holiday, they find that they are running out of money. They ask the holiday representative if she can organise the transfer of some money, to cover their expenses for the remainder of the stay. John's mother agrees to provide the funds and the representative arranges the transfer of money from the UK.

DISCUSSION POINTS

1. How would you have avoided John's and Susan's problems?

2. Which questions would you want to ask the holiday representative regarding any aspect of your holiday?

3. Are there any improvements which could be made to the representative's work which you feel would benefit holidaymakers? If so what are they?

14
Dealing with Complaints and Claims

MAKING COMPLAINTS ABROAD

Everybody hopes that their holiday will go smoothly with no causes for complaint. However, this is not always the case, and it is as well to know what to do if things do go wrong and you need to complain.

The most common complaint on package holidays tend to be:

- dissatisfaction with hotel/apartment including things not working
- booked and paid for a sea view room but have not been given one
- activities/services/amenities advertised in the brochure not available
- dissatisfaction with hotel food
- dissatisfaction with excursions booked through holiday representative
- overbooking at chosen hotel.

Reporting your complaint

Whatever your reason for complaint, you must report it to your holiday representative at the first opportunity. If they can sort out your complaint, they will usually do their best to do so.

Whether it is resolved or not they will ask you to complete a complaint form. You write down the nature of your complaint and then sign it at the bottom, along with the representative's signature and date. They will state on the form whether it has been resolved, or whether you will be continuing with it upon your return to the UK. You keep your copy, the representative keeps theirs, and they advise head office in the UK of the complaint.

If you do not lodge this initial complaint and obtain the relevant report form, you will not be able to follow it up if necessary once you return home. Any claims for compensation will be ignored.

Dealing with overbooking

If you arrive at your destination airport only to be told by the holiday representative that your hotel is overbooked, the following advice may be of use:

- Make sure you take your holiday confirmation with you, as this will state the type of room or apartment you have booked.

- Make sure that the tour operator pays for any transport expenses to the alternative hotel or apartment.

- If you are moved to a more expensive hotel, make sure that you have it in writing that the tour operator will pay for any extra expense.

- Do not accept any compensation from the tour operator until you have seen the alternative hotel/apartment and are satisfied with it.

- Take the relevant page of the brochure with you showing the amenities available, then you can make sure the alternative has similar if not better facilities than the original.

- State exactly what you want in an overbooking situation. People who make a fuss will probably be placed in nicer accommodation to avoid future problems. The meek and mild will be positioned wherever suits the tour operator.

- Try and find out from the representative or hotel when the overbooking problem arose, as this could make a difference if pursuing the complaint afterwards.

- Make notes of all the inconvenience to yourself and advise the tour operator via your travel agent in writing on your return.

FOLLOWING UP COMPLAINTS

If your complaint was not sorted out satisfactorily while you were on holiday, you will need to follow it up on your return.

Using your travel agent
You will get better results if you sort out the complaint via your travel agent, rather than deal with the tour operator directly yourself.

Once you have returned from your holiday, you have 28 days to inform the tour operator of your intention to continue with the complaint. Go and see the travel agent, who will tell you to provide the following things:

- a full letter from yourself detailing the reason for complaint
- the complaint report form issued in the resort by the holiday representative
- any evidence you have to support your complaint.

Evidence to support your complaint can be in the form of video film, photographs, and names and addresses of other fellow holidaymakers who share your complaint and will support you.

Once you have provided the travel agent with the required items, they will usually enclose a letter from themselves regarding the complaint, and quoting the booking reference for your holiday, which the tour operator requires to deal with the complaint.

Photocopies of all paperwork should be taken before forwarding them to the tour operator.

Accepting what is offered

Once the tour operator receives all the reports and evidence, they will reply to your complaint via your travel agent within 28 days. Initially they may just offer an explanation. If you are not satisfied and feel you are entitled to be compensated, advise the travel agent of your wishes. They will probably ask you to provide a further letter as they can only act on your instructions.

You need to be firm about your complaint, advising the tour operator that you intend to take matters further if a satisfactory settlement is not reached.

After several exchanges of letters, they may make an offer of compensation. If you are happy to accept this then all well and good. If not, push for more compensation. If you still feel that the settlement is not reasonable, you can take matters further.

TAKING MATTERS FURTHER

If the complaint cannot be settled amicably, ABTA offer an arbitration scheme, which is administered independently by the Chartered Institute of Arbitrators. Your travel agent should be able to obtain an application form for you. If you prefer you can obtain one from ABTA's Consumer Affairs Department (see Useful Addresses).

The system cannot be used:

● for claims for more than £1500 per person or £7500 per booking
● for complaints involving illness or injury (physical)
● if you contact them more than nine months after you return from holiday.

The service aims to provide:

● an inexpensive and simple way of sorting out your complaints
● a limit on the costs that may have to be paid

- a final decision which is based on documents only, so you do not have to appear in person. It is therefore in your interests to provide as much evidence as possible to support your complaint.

Alternatively, you can deal with your complaint through the courts.

MAKING INSURANCE CLAIMS

If anything goes wrong on holiday which is claimable through your holiday insurance, then you should be aware of the procedure to follow.

Supporting your claim

No matter what you are claiming for, if you do not have the evidence to support your claim, the insurance company will not pay out. Figure 17 shows the evidence required for the different types of insurance claim.

Obtaining a claims form

As soon as you return from holiday, advise your travel agent of your need to claim and they should apply for a claims form for you. They sometimes have them in stock for the independent insurance which they sell.

Booking direct
If you have booked your holiday direct with the tour operator, you will need to phone them for a claims form and sort the claim out yourself.

Completing the form

When you complete the form make sure:

- you have the correct claims form for the claim you are making, as there are several different forms

- you complete it fully: your travel agent will probably be able to advise you on any questions which you are unsure about

- you sign the declaration and date it.

Failure to answer all the questions will only delay settlement of the claim. If your travel agent obtained your claims form, it will lead to less confusion if he sends the completed form off for you. Make sure photocopies are taken of all correspondence before sending it off.

If you have a claim which requires your GP to complete part of the form, the GP is entitled to charge you for doing so.

Type of claim	Evidence required by insurance company
Damaged baggage	Report from airline as soon as it is noticed. Baggage tags stapled to flight ticket. Estimate from repairers on return. Photographs of case (optional).
Delayed baggage	Property Irregularity Report issued at airport. Baggage tags stapled to your flight ticket. Receipts for all purchases made due to no luggage.
Stolen property	Police report detailing nature of robbery and items stolen. Report from representative if you cannot obtain police report. List of stolen property and estimated replacement value. Invoice for replacement passport if stolen.
Medical claims	Receipts for any medicines, drugs, doctors fees, medical treatment charged for while abroad. Invoices for any outstanding amounts not settled.
Travel delay	Report from tour operator/airline stating actual times flight departed and arrived and total length of delay.
Cancellation/ curtailment	Death certificate if due to death of close relative. Completed medical form from GP if due to illness. Proof of being required for jury service. Proof of redundancy (if covered) letter from employers.

Fig. 17. Table showing evidence required for insurance claims.

Providing the necessary documentation

Once you have completed the claims form, you need to collect all the necessary documentation together, which is in addition to the evidence required in Figure 17, in order to submit your claim to the insurance company.

Normally they require the following regardless of what your claim is for:

- fully completed claims form
- original insurance certificate
- travel agent's invoice for holiday
- tour operator's invoice.

Submitting the claim

Take photocopies of the documents and of your evidence before sending your claim. Some insurance companies will acknowledge receipt of your claim, some won't.

Chasing them up

Do not expect a settlement within a couple of weeks. Even the most straightforward of claims can take weeks to settle. The insurance companies are never in a hurry to pay out.

However, if you have not heard from them after a number of weeks, and your travel agent dealt with your claim, ask him to chase them up. He will probably get further with them than if you deal with them yourself.

CHECKLIST

- Have you reported your complaint to the holiday representative?
- Have you been given a copy of the complaints form?
- Have both you and the holiday representative signed the form?
- Are you aware of the advice given regarding overbooking?
- Have you collected evidence to support your complaint?
- Have you followed your complaint up on your return home?
- Have you taken matters further if you are not happy with the offer?
- Have you kept reports, receipts, bills to support your claim?
- Have you obtained a claims form on your return home?
- Have you checked you have the correct form for your claim?
- Have you completed the form fully?
- Have you signed the declaration at the end of the form?
- Have you enclosed all the evidence for your claim?
- Have you enclosed the other necessary documentation?
- Have photocopies been taken of everything you are submitting?
- Have you chased the claim up if it is taking a long time?

CASE STUDIES

Edward's and Jean's insurance claim

Despite the fact that Edward and Jean changed tour operator a month before their departure date due to an overbooking problem with the original one, they have no cause for complaint whilst on holiday.

Edward falls ill and expenses are incurred as a result of seeing the doctor twice and for medication.

Upon their return they inform the travel agent of the claim, and a form is applied for. Edward has kept all the relevant receipts and documentation to support his claim.

Nancy's missing suitcase

Upon arrival at Crete airport, Nancy realises that her suitcase is missing. She informs the holiday representative, who helps her complete the relevant forms. The following day there is still no sign of the case, so she has to buy essentials.

Nancy very wisely keeps receipts and makes a list of all her necessary purchases to support her insurance claim. She has kept her baggage tags stuck to her ticket from when the suitcase was checked-in.

The suitcase finally appears on the fifth day of her holiday, having visited three other Greek islands. She has no complaints about the hotel or her holiday and enjoys it all the more once her suitcase arrives.

Once home, she returns to the travel agent, who helps her with the claim for the delayed suitcase.

John's and Susan's disaster

As John and Susan took up a special offer they had no control over which resort or accommodation they would be placed in. They end up in an apartment with no facilities for the children and a long way from the beach. The resort is very small and has three bars, a couple of restaurants and a supermarket.

When the holiday representative visits the apartments, John demands to be moved elsewhere. As it is the height of the season moving is not possible. She explains that he is on a special offer and so does not really have grounds for complaint.

John intends to follow the complaint up on his return and so completes a complaints form whilst on holiday.

Once home he goes into the travel agents and makes a scene about his disaster of a holiday. They advise him to put his complaints into writing and that they will send them off on his behalf. They point out that he did book a special offer.

DISCUSSION POINTS

1. Do you feel that John and Susan are justified in complaining about their holiday? If so why?

2. What improvements would you make to the complaints system for holidays?

3. Before reading this chapter, which aspects of insurance claims were you aware of? What steps do you think should be taken to make other holidaymakers aware of insurance claims generally?

WELL, WHAT DID YOU EXPECT ON "BUCKET AIR"?

Glossary

Agent's discounts. Incentives offered by travel agents to encourage you to book with them.

All inclusive holiday. All meals, local drinks, entertainment and some sports are included in the cost.

Amendment fees. Charges made as a result of altering your holiday.

Aparthotel. Self catering accommodation with the option to have meals at extra cost.

Arbitration scheme. Way of settling claims/complaints out of court when an agreement cannot be reached.

Association of British Travel Agents. The body which lays down the rules governing the travel industry and ensures they are adhered to.

Availability. Which holidays are available upon checking via the computer.

Balance. The amount left to pay on your holiday after the deposit has been deducted.

Basic cost. Cost of holiday before any supplements are added.

Board supplements. Charges made for any extra meals required.

Booking conditions. Rules laid down when booking a holiday to protect both the customer and tour operator.

Booking direct. Booking with the tour operator not through a travel agent.

Cancellation charges. Charges made as a result of cancelling your holiday.

Chartered Institute of Arbitrators. Body responsible for the governing of the arbitration scheme offered by ABTA.

Code of Conduct. Rules laid down by ABTA which tour operators and travel agents must abide by.

Commission. What a travel agent earns for booking your holiday.

Confirming holidays. Advising the travel agent of your wish to definitely book the holiday, which is done via the computer.

Costing. A breakdown of the different prices of your holiday.

Curtailment. Cutting the holiday short.

Deposit. Payment made when booking your holiday to secure it.

Excess waiver. A supplement payable upon taking insurance out, so that excesses do not have to be paid in the event of a claim.

Facilities. Things which are included or are available such as bath, shower, WC, balcony in hotel room.

Family insurance policy. An insurance where adults and children are covered for one price rather than charged individually.

Financial protection. Protection provided by ABTA members in the event of a company failing financially.

Flight supplement. Charge made for flights from regional airports with better timings and departure days.

Flight timings. Proposed departure and arrival times for your holiday flights.

Foreign travellers cheques. Travellers cheques in the currency of the country you are travelling to.

Holding options. Travel agents can hold a holiday for 24 hours to enable you to decide if you require it.

Holiday duration. Length of your holiday stay.

Holiday invoice. Bill issued by the tour operator showing a breakdown of the holiday cost.

Indemnity forms. Form which must be signed when you are given a low deposit offer, which states you will pay the remaining deposit by a certain date.

Infant. Chjld under the age of two on the return date of the holiday.

Insurance excesses. The amount which must be paid by you in the event of a claim.

Insurance exclusions. Things which are not covered by the insurance.

Insurance policy. Document issued when holiday insurance is taken out.

Insurance premiums. Price you pay to take out holiday insurance.

International Driving Permit. Document required when hiring a car in Spain or Italy, if you have an old style green driving licence.

Legal advice and expenses. Insurance cover for expenses incurred as a result of obtaining compensation because of the insured person's death or injury.

Official rating. Rating given to properties by the tourist authority of individual countries.

Personal liability. Insurance to cover accidentally injuring someone or damaging someone else's property.

Property Irregularity Report. Form to be completed when baggage is lost or damaged.

Regional airport. Your local or nearest airport.

Resort transfers. Journey usually by coach from the airport to your holiday resort.

Restricted currencies. Currencies which are not allowed to be taken into or out of that country.

Silent airports. Airports which do not announce flight departures, but display information on computer screens.

Single room supplement. Extra charge made for one person occupying a hotel room.

Special requests. Requests made at the time of booking for your holiday.

Topping and tailing. When two children share a bed to save space in a hotel room.

Tour operator. Company whose brochure you book your holiday from.

Tour operator's rating. Rating given by tour operators to hotels and apartments which they feature in their brochures.

Travel agent. Person who sells holidays on the tour operator's behalf.

Umbrella ABTA numbers. Travel agents using another travel agent's ABTA number because they have not got one.

Visa. Document required by some countries to gain entry.

Welcome meeting. Get-together held at the start of the holiday organised by the holiday representative.

Useful Addresses

GENERAL TRAVEL INFORMATION

The Automobile Association, Norfolk House, Priestley Road, Basingstoke, Hampshire RG24 9NY., Tel: (0990) 500600.

The Foreign & Commonwealth Office, Travel advice unit, Consular division, 1 Palace Street, London SW1E 5HE. Tel: (0171) 270 4129.

HEALTH MATTERS

British Airways travel clinics. Tel: (0171) 831 5333. Phone for nearest centre, 40 centres in total. Advice and vaccination services.

Department of Health, Richmond House, 79 Whitehall, London SW1A 2NS. Tel: (0171) 210 4850.

LEGAL MATTERS

The Association of British Travel Agents (ABTA), Consumer Affairs Department, 55-57 Newman Street, London W1P 4AH. Tel: (0171) 307 1907. Advice on complaints/arbitration service.

The Chartered Institute of Arbitrators, International Arbitration Centre, 24 Angel Gate, City Road, London EC1V 2RS. Tel: (0171) 837 4483.

PASSPORT OFFICES

Hampton House, 47-53 High Street, Belfast BT1 2QS. Tel: (01232) 232371.

3 Northgate, 96 Milton Street, Cowcaddens, Glasgow G4 0BT. Tel: (0141) 332 0271.

5th floor India Buildings, Water Street, Liverpool L2 0QZ. Tel: (0151) 237 3010.

Clive House, 70 Petty France, London SW1H 9HD. Tel: (0171) 799 2290.

Olympia House, Upper Dock Street, Newport, Gwent NP9 1XA. Tel: (01633) 244500.

Aragon Court, Northminster Road, Peterborough PE1 1QG. Tel: (01733) 895555.

TOURIST OFFICES

Cyprus Tourism Organisation, 213 Regent Street, London W1R 8DA. Tel: (0171) 734 9822.

National Tourist Office, Gambia High Commission, 57 Kensington Court, London W8 5DG. Tel: (0171) 937 6316.

Gibraltar Information Bureau, Arundel Great Court, 179 The Strand, London WC2R 1EH. Tel: (0171) 836 0777.

The Greek National Tourist Office, 4 Conduit Street, London W1R 0DJ. Tel: (0171) 734 5997.

The Italian State Tourist Office, 1 Princes Street, London W1R 8AY. Tel: (0171) 408 1254.

Malta Tourist Office, Malta House, 36-38 Piccadilly, London W1V 0PP. Tel: (0171) 292 4900.

Portuguese National Tourist Office, 22-25a Sackville Street, London W1X 1DE. Tel: (0171) 494 1441.

Spanish National Tourist Office, 57-58 St James Street, London SW1A 1LD. Tel: (0171) 499 0901.

Tunisian National Tourist Office, 77a Wigmore Street, London W1H 9LJ. Tel: (0171) 224 5561.

The Turkish Tourist Office, 1st floor, Egyptian House, 170-173 Piccadilly, London W1V 9DD. Tel: (0171) 629 7771.

Further Reading

BOOKS

Good Health, Good Travel, Ted Lankester (Hodder & Stoughton).
How to Take Great Trips with Your Kids, Sanford Portnoy and Joan Flynn Portnoy (The Harvard Common Press).
Making a Complaint, Helen Shay (How to Books).

LEAFLETS

British Consular Services Abroad, Foreign and Commonwealth Office.
Checklist for Travellers, Foreign and Commonwealth Office.
Do's and Don'ts in . . ., Foreign and Commonwealth Office, 25 different countries covered.
Health Advice for Travellers, leaflet T5, Department of Health.
Healthwise for Travellers, leaflet T4, Department of Health.
Holiday Guide for Families, Thomas Cook.
Late Holiday Resort Cards, Thomas Cook: cards on the popular resorts which provide maps, temperature charts and resort information.
What Should You Look For When Booking Your Holiday?, The Association of British Travel Agents. Explaining the importance of ABTA.

MAGAZINES

BBC Holidays, BBC Magazines, 101 Bayham Street, London NW1 0AG.
Good Holiday Magazine, 91 High Street, Esher, Surrey KT10 9QD.
Holiday Which?, 2 Marylebone Road, London NW1 4DF.

Index

HOW TO GET A JOB IN TRAVEL & TOURISM
An international guide to employment opportunities

Mark Hempshell

Would you enjoy working in travel and tourism? Do you already have a local position, but want to venture overseas? Whatever your age, background or qualifications, this book will open doors for you. With lots of examples, it shows how and where to obtain really great jobs as couriers, holiday reps, coach drivers, tour guides, entertainers, sports instructors or airline staff. Or how about working on cruise ships, in top hotels and restaurants, on safaris, summer camps, winter sports or other exotic assignments? The book tells you what each job involves, the skills, qualifications, experience, language, training, permits, pay and conditions – plus where to find vacancies and how to apply. Someone has to do all these glamorous jobs – use this book, and it could be you! Mark Hempshell's other books include *Your Own Business in Europe*, *How to Get a Job in Hotels & Catering*, *How to Get a Job in Europe* and *How to Get a Job in France*, and others in this series.

160pp illus. 1 85703 212 8. 2nd edition.

HOW TO EMIGRATE
Your complete guide to a successful future overseas

Roger Jones

Would you like to pack your bags, and make a completely new life for yourself overseas? According to a recent poll, thousands of people would, dreaming of a better lifestyle, new horizons and a more rewarding future. But how do you actually go about it? Which countries should you consider, and what visas and permits will you need? In practical steps, this book will set you on the right path, with essential advice and information on weighing up your prospects, choosing the right location, coping with immigration, the actual move, housing, employment and settling in successfully to your new life overseas. Written by a leading writer of books on living and working overseas. 'Very practical and entertaining – I would recommend it.' *Phoenix/Association of Graduate Careers Advisory Services.*

176pp illus. 1 85703 101 6.

WORKING AS A HOLIDAY REP
How to have the time of your life working around the world

Steve Marks

The package holiday industry is one of the success stories of recent years with millions of people now holidaying abroad each year. The holiday representative or 'Rep' is in charge of making every guest's stay a problem-free and enjoyable one. This book explains how to join the growing army of reps who work in holiday resorts worldwide, summer and winter. Within its pages you'll discover what qualities are looked for in would-be reps, what the work involves and how to apply for vacancies together with a listing of the companies who employ reps at home and abroad. If you'd like an exciting new career, offering the opportunity for world travel, and good pay too, then this book is most definitely for you. Steve Marks is a freelance travel author and journalist. He has worked for Thompson and Airtours, and contributed travel features to *Overseas Jobs Express* and other newspapers and magazines.

128pp. illus. 1 85703 330 2.

MAKING A COMPLAINT
How to put your case successfully and win redress

Helen Shay

Whether you've bought faulty shoes or been sold an unsuitable investment; been over-charged by a bank or suffered the holiday from hell; this book guides you through the maze of complaints procedures, courts, ombudsmen and other forms of consumer redress. It makes the law user-friendly and shows you how to obtain compensation – fast. It shows the way to cut through the aggravation and achieve the best solution for you. Helen Shay is a solicitor of twelve years' standing. She has worked both in private practice and as an in-house lawyer for a major high street retailer – so has experience of consumer disputes from both sides. Currently with an ombudsman's office, she is well versed in current consumer issues and the problems which can confront the individual versus large organisations. She also tutors and lectures part-time in commercial law, and is knowledgeable in contract, consumer credit, banking law, conveyancing and other legal areas affecting everyday life.

116pp. illus. 1 85703 102 4.

WORKING ON CRUISE SHIPS
How to have the time of your life working around the world

Steve Marks

Would you enjoy working on board a luxury cruise ship? It's the ideal way to see the world, working as you go, and earning a good salary (plus tips) too. There are hundreds of different jobs to do on board every cruise ship including cabin staff, waiters and waitresses, chefs, kitchen hands, bar staff, deck hands, hairdressers, singers, dancers and musicians, sports instructors and casino staff. The cruise industry is expanding rapidly with hundreds of exciting, well paid positions to be filled every month. This book describes the jobs available, explains how to apply and gives details of all the main employers who recruit for careers on board ship. Steve Marks is a freelance travel author and journalist. He has worked for Cunard, and contributed travel features to *Overseas Jobs Express* and other newspapers and magazines.

128pp. illus. 1 85703 335 3.

HOW TO TRAVEL ROUND THE WORLD
Your practical guide to the experience of a lifetime

Nick Vandome

Fed up with the situation back home? Want to have some fun, adventure and excitement? Then this is the book for you. Written by a travel writer with extensive first-hand knowledge, this book explains how to prepare for a real globetrotting adventure, how to plan your itinerary, how to organise passports, visa permits and other international paperwork, how to plan your means of travel, kitting yourself out, planning for health and safety on the move, learning to live with different languages and cultures, earning as you go, trouble shooting, and more. The book is complete with a gazetteer of international travel information, case studies, contacts for travel, health and work, further reading, and index. Go for it – and give yourself the experience of a lifetime.

224pp illus. 1 85703 121 0.

MANAGING YOUR PERSONAL FINANCES
How to achieve financial security and survive the shrinking welfare state

John Claxton

Life for most people has become increasingly beset by financial worries, and meanwhile the once-dependable prop of state help is shrinking. Today's financial world is a veritable jungle full of predators after your money. This book will help you to check your financial health and prepare a strategy towards creating your own welfare state and financial independence. Find out in simple language with many examples and case studies how to avoid debt, how to finance your home, how to prepare for possible incapacity or redundancy and how to finance your retirement, including care in old age. Discover how to acquire new financial skills, increase your income, reduce outgoings, and prepare to survive in a more self-reliant world. John Claxton is a chartered management accountant and chartered secretary; he teaches personal money management in adult education.

160pp. illus. 1 85703 328 0.

HOW TO RETIRE ABROAD
Your guide to successful planning and decision making

Roger Jones

Increasing numbers of people are looking for opportunities to base their retirement overseas – away from many of the hassles of life in the UK. Written by a specialist in expatriate matters, this handbook will guide you successfully step-by-step through the whole process of finding a new home, coping with key matters such as tax, foreign investment, property, health care, and even working overseas. The book is complete with a country-by-country guide. 'All you need to know about retiring in the country of your choice.' *Destination New Zealand.* 'Anyone even thinking of retiring overseas would find it money well spent.' *Corona Worldwide.* Roger Jones is a freelance author specialising in expatriate information. His other books include *How to Get a Job Abroad, How to Teach Abroad* and *How to Get a Job in America.* He has himself lived and worked extensively overseas.

176pp. 1 85703 051 6.

How To Books

How To Books provide practical help on a large range of topics. They are available through all good bookshops or can be ordered direct from the distributors. Just tick the titles you want and complete the form on the following page.

___ Apply to an Industrial Tribunal (£7.99)
___ Applying for a Job (£7.99)
___ Applying for a United States Visa (£15.99)
___ Be a Freelance Journalist (£8.99)
___ Be a Freelance Secretary (£8.99)
___ Be a Local Councillor (£8.99)
___ Be an Effective School Governor (£9.99)
___ Become a Freelance Sales Agent (£9.99)
___ Become an Au Pair (£8.99)
___ Buy & Run a Shop (£8.99)
___ Buy & Run a Small Hotel (£8.99)
___ Cash from your Computer (£9.99)
___ Career Planning for Women (£8.99)
___ Choosing a Nursing Home (£8.99)
___ Claim State Benefits (£9.99)
___ Communicate at Work (£7.99)
___ Conduct Staff Appraisals (£7.99)
___ Conducting Effective Interviews (£8.99)
___ Copyright & Law for Writers (£8.99)
___ Counsel People at Work (£7.99)
___ Creating a Twist in the Tale (£8.99)
___ Creative Writing (£9.99)
___ Critical Thinking for Students (£8.99)
___ Do Voluntary Work Abroad (£8.99)
___ Do Your Own Advertising (£8.99)
___ Do Your Own PR (£8.99)
___ Doing Business Abroad (£9.99)
___ Emigrate (£9.99)
___ Employ & Manage Staff (£8.99)
___ Find Temporary Work Abroad (£8.99)
___ Finding a Job in Canada (£9.99)
___ Finding a Job in Computers (£8.99)
___ Finding a Job in New Zealand (£9.99)
___ Finding a Job with a Future (£8.99)
___ Finding Work Overseas (£9.99)
___ Freelance DJ-ing (£8.99)
___ Get a Job Abroad (£10.99)
___ Get a Job in America (£9.99)
___ Get a Job in Australia (£9.99)
___ Get a Job in Europe (£9.99)
___ Get a Job in France (£9.99)
___ Get a Job in Germany (£9.99)
___ Get a Job in Hotels and Catering (£8.99)
___ Get a Job in Travel & Tourism (£8.99)
___ Get into Films & TV (£8.99)
___ Get into Radio (£8.99)
___ Get That Job (£6.99)
___ Getting your First Job (£8.99)
___ Going to University (£8.99)
___ Helping your Child to Read (£8.99)
___ Investing in People (£8.99)
___ Invest in Stocks & Shares (£8.99)

___ Keep Business Accounts (£7.99)
___ Know Your Rights at Work (£8.99)
___ Know Your Rights: Teachers (£6.99)
___ Live & Work in America (£9.99)
___ Live & Work in Australia (£12.99)
___ Live & Work in Germany (£9.99)
___ Live & Work in Greece (£9.99)
___ Live & Work in Italy (£8.99)
___ Live & Work in New Zealand (£9.99)
___ Live & Work in Portugal (£9.99)
___ Live & Work in Spain (£7.99)
___ Live & Work in the Gulf (£9.99)
___ Living & Working in Britain (£8.99)
___ Living & Working in China (£9.99)
___ Living & Working in Hong Kong (£10.99)
___ Living & Working in Israel (£10.99)
___ Living & Working in Japan (£8.99)
___ Living & Working in Saudi Arabia (£12.99)
___ Living & Working in the Netherlands (£9.99)
___ Lose Weight & Keep Fit (£6.99)
___ Make a Wedding Speech (£7.99)
___ Making a Complaint (£8.99)
___ Manage a Sales Team (£8.99)
___ Manage an Office (£8.99)
___ Manage Computers at Work (£8.99)
___ Manage People at Work (£8.99)
___ Manage Your Career (£8.99)
___ Managing Budgets & Cash Flows (£9.99)
___ Managing Meetings (£8.99)
___ Managing Your Personal Finances (£8.99)
___ Market Yourself (£8.99)
___ Master Book-Keeping (£8.99)
___ Mastering Business English (£8.99)
___ Master GCSE Accounts (£8.99)
___ Master Languages (£8.99)
___ Master Public Speaking (£8.99)
___ Obtaining Visas & Work Permits (£9.99)
___ Organising Effective Training (£9.99)
___ Pass Exams Without Anxiety (£7.99)
___ Pass That Interview (£6.99)
___ Plan a Wedding (£7.99)
___ Prepare a Business Plan (£8.99)
___ Publish a Book (£9.99)
___ Publish a Newsletter (£9.99)
___ Raise Funds & Sponsorship (£7.99)
___ Rent & Buy Property in France (£9.99)
___ Rent & Buy Property in Italy (£9.99)
___ Retire Abroad (£8.99)
___ Return to Work (£7.99)
___ Run a Local Campaign (£6.99)
___ Run a Voluntary Group (£8.99)
___ Sell Your Business (£9.99)

___ Selling into Japan (£14.99)
___ Setting up Home in Florida (£9.99)
___ Spend a Year Abroad (£8.99)
___ Start a Business from Home (£7.99)
___ Start a New Career (£6.99)
___ Starting to Manage (£8.99)
___ Starting to Write (£8.99)
___ Start Word Processing (£8.99)
___ Start Your Own Business (£8.99)
___ Study Abroad (£8.99)
___ Study & Learn (£7.99)
___ Study & Live in Britain (£7.99)
___ Studying at University (£8.99)
___ Studying for a Degree (£8.99)
___ Successful Grandparenting (£8.99)
___ Successful Mail Order Marketing (£9.99)
___ Successful Single Parenting (£8.99)
___ Survive at College (£4.99)
___ Survive Divorce (£8.99)
___ Surviving Redundancy (£8.99)
___ Take Care of Your Heart (£5.99)
___ Taking in Students (£8.99)
___ Taking on Staff (£8.99)
___ Taking Your A-Levels (£8.99)
___ Teach Abroad (£8.99)
___ Teach Adults (£8.99)
___ Teaching Someone to Drive (£8.99)
___ Travel Round the World (£8.99)
___ Use a Library (£6.99)

___ Use the Internet (£9.99)
___ Winning Consumer Competitions (£8.99)
___ Winning Presentations (£8.99)
___ Work from Home (£8.99)
___ Work in an Office (£7.99)
___ Work in Retail (£8.99)
___ Work with Dogs (£8.99)
___ Working Abroad (£14.99)
___ Working as a Holiday Rep (£9.99)
___ Working in Japan (£10.99)
___ Working in Photography (£8.99)
___ Working in the Gulf (£10.99)
___ Working on Contract Worldwide (£9.99)
___ Working on Cruise Ships (£9.99)
___ Write a CV that Works (£7.99)
___ Write a Press Release (£9.99)
___ Write a Report (£8.99)
___ Write an Assignment (£8.99)
___ Write an Essay (£7.99)
___ Write & Sell Computer Software (£9.99)
___ Write Business Letters (£8.99)
___ Write for Publication (£8.99)
___ Write for Television (£8.99)
___ Write Your Dissertation (£8.99)
___ Writing a Non Fiction Book (£8.99)
___ Writing & Selling a Novel (£8.99)
___ Writing & Selling Short Stories (£8.99)
___ Writing Reviews (£8.99)
___ Your Own Business in Europe (£12.99)

To: Plymbridge Distributors Ltd, Plymbridge House, Estover Road, Plymouth PL6 7PZ. Customer Services Tel: (01752) 202301. Fax: (01752) 202331.

Please send me copies of the titles I have indicated. Please add postage & packing (UK £1, Europe including Eire, £2, World £3 airmail).

☐ I enclose cheque/PO payable to Plymbridge Distributors Ltd for £ _____

☐ Please charge to my ☐ MasterCard, ☐ Visa, ☐ AMEX card.

Account No. ☐☐☐☐☐☐☐☐☐☐☐☐☐☐☐☐

Card Expiry Date ☐ 19 ☐   ☎ **Credit Card orders may be faxed or phoned.**

Customer Name (CAPITALS) ....

Address ....

.... Postcode ....

Telephone .... Signature ....

Every effort will be made to despatch your copy as soon as possible but to avoid possible disappointment please allow up to 21 days for despatch time (42 days if overseas). Prices and availability are subject to change without notice.

Code BPA